Gardening
Month by Month
in Northern California

Bob Tanem
Don Williamson

Lone Pine Publishing

© 2004 by Lone Pine Publishing
First printed in 2004   10 9 8 7 6 5 4 3 2 1
Printed in Canada

The Publisher: Lone Pine Publishing

10145 – 81 Avenue	1808 B Street NW, Suite 140
Edmonton, AB T6E 1W9 Canada	Auburn, WA, USA 98001

Website: www.lonepinepublishing.com

National Library of Canada Cataloguing in Publication Data
Tanem, Bob, 1930–
    Gardening month by month in Northern California / Bob Tanem, Don Williamson.

    ISBN 1-55105-365-9

    1. Gardening—California, Northern. I. Williamson, Don, 1962–II. Title.
SB453.2.C3T35 2003   635'.09794   C2003-905268-0

Editorial Director: Nancy Foulds
Project Editor: Sandra Bit
Researchers: Don Williamson, Laura Peters
Production Manager: Gene Longson
Book Design & Layout: Heather Markham
Maps & Climate Charts: Elliot Engley, Chia-Jung Chang
Cover Design: Gerry Dotto
Principal Photographers: Tamara Eder, Tim Matheson, Kim Patrick O'Leary
Illustrations: Ian Sheldon
Scanning, Separations & Film: Elite Lithographers Co.

Front cover photographs (clockwise from top right): by Tamara Eder, geum 'Lady Stratheden', *Ligularia dentata,* sweet potato vine 'Terrace Lime', geum, hybrid tea rose 'Garden Party', 'Teddy Bear' sunflower; *by Kim O'Leary,* alstroemeria; *by Tim Matheson,* daylily, dahlia, Japanese kerria.

All other photos: All-American Selections 99c, 120–121; Linda Oyama Bryan 67a, 81a; Joan de Grey 154; Therese D'Monte 70; Don Doucette 15b; Elliot Engley 31c, 33a,b&c; Jennifer Fafard 123b, 129d, 151b; Derek Fell 35c, 55a, 125c, 135c, 143b; Erika Flatt 65c, 117a, 149a&d; Anne Gordon 137a; Saxon Holt 12–13, 15a, 16, 24–25, 27a, 39a, 45a, 48–49, 63b, 72–73, 81d, 83a, 108–109, 111b, 113a, 123a, 125b, 132–133, 135b, 144–145, 147a&b, 150, 151a, 155a&b; Horticolor©Nova-Photographik/Horticolor 94; Colin Laroque 96–97; Heather Markham 75a; Marilynn McAra 36–37, 42, 43b&c, 55d, 115a,b&c; Alison Penko 27c, 38, 113b; Laura Peters 119c, 141d; Robert Ritchie 117b; Peter Thompstone 51c, 53a, 57b; Mark Turner 35d, 124; Don Williamson 119a

Hardiness zones map: based on the USDA Plant Hardiness Zones map; *Climate charts & precipitation map:* data used with permission from the Western Regional Climate Center website, http://www.wrcc.dri.edu/COMPARATIVE.html.

We acknowledge the financial support of the Government of Canada through the Book Publishing Industry Development Program (BPIDP) for our publishing activities.

PC: 01

There is only one way to describe gardening in Northern California: wonderful. Our different soils, seasonal variations, altitudes and variety of plant materials make our gardens unique. Microclimates in the hot interior valleys allow plant materials that normally thrive only in coastal areas to grow successfully. Conversely, some tropical plants that require heat, such as bougainvillea, are extremely successful in some of the foggiest areas of San Francisco and Carmel.

blue-bean (*Decaisnea fargesii*) arching over path

Northern California's temperate climate supports a wide array of growing conditions. In coastal areas, summers are usually cool and winters are mild, but persistent fog in summer can be a problem. Protecting plants from winds that regularly bring in fog is another must. Summers in the interior valleys are typically baking hot and winters are cold enough to provide dormancy for perennials and flowering shrubs to set flowers for next year. The valleys are foggy during the winter (November through January), with an average temperature of 42°F. Fog is not usually a problem in the coastal mountains or the Sierra foothills, and warmer days and cooler nights are common in winter. Northeast and mountainous regions have short, dry summers and cold winters. Because of these temperature differences, annuals, perennials and other plants needing hot summers and cold winters, such as peonies, lilacs and most deciduous fruit trees, do especially well here. Each region offers unique challenges to the gardener. One factor is consistent, however: precipitation is rare in all regions from the end of March to the middle of October. Humidity is not usually a problem except in areas where summer fog persists daily.

agave and other succulents

xeriscape planting

Gardening at higher altitudes poses special challenges. The growing season is short, summers are cool and winters are freezing. Always check your seed catalogs for hardiness before planting. Vegetables such as tomatoes, peppers and green beans may not work except with special attention. But don't despair; other vegetables grow well in a shorter season, so you can enjoy their garden-fresh taste. The soil in the Sierra mountains, with its glacial deposits of clay and granite, combines the advantages of water retention and proper drainage, permitting a variety of cold-hardy perennials, trees and shrubs to work well in your garden year after year.

The key to gardening success is the temperature of the soil. Rarely does the soil temperature in coastal areas dip below 48°F. Although summertime temperatures are higher in foothill gardens bordering the Central Valley, the constant fog has a cooling effect. The farther you move away from the coastline, the less effect this cooling will have. The soil temperatures will vary, and in many of these areas, winter frost will cool the soil to freezing, which kills tropical plants but enables fruit trees to produce more fruit than

formal plantings and topiary at Filoli

they do in warmer coastal environs. As you use this monthly guide, consult the climate charts and maps on pp. 8–11 for an indication of typical climate conditions in your area.

Your soil and what you do with it are a second key to success. Heavy brown clay is in all cases rich in nutrients, but as it dries out in the summer, it also becomes so hard that the roots of many plants cannot penetrate it to take advantage of the richness of the soil. Clay soil is common in all parts of Northern California. The exception is near the coast, or where the ocean influence has been most prevalent. In these areas, the soil is composed largely of sand and drains so quickly that its nutrients are rapidly depleted. Unless plants have unusually deep roots, they

gazanias

pine & lantern (*above*), bonsai juniper & spruce (*below*)

Japanese maple shading water feature (*below*)

won't survive. However, don't let sandy soil stop you from gardening. Adding plenty of organic matter and mulch improves nutrient retention. A well-known example of plants growing in sandy soil is Golden Gate Park, which was landscaped on sand dunes. The sand's high salt content had to be leached out before the area could be planted.

Serpentine soil, composed of layers of impenetrable rock mixed with layers of clay, was formed by the upheaval of the ocean floor that today forms the coastal mountain range. Serpentine soil is similar to clay and requires the same treatment with organic matter, fertilization and mulching. Unlike clay soil, serpentine soil can have limited nutrients because of the presence of toxic metals. It should be mixed with 50% planting mix. Serpentine soil has the advantage of fractures in the strata that allow for root growth. This fracturing helps anchor trees and shrubs.

The warmth of the Central Valley tends to influence the temperature in the Sierra foothills. Remarkably, the soil profile changes to one of rich loam and very little clay in the valleys and decomposed granite and clay in the foothills. The treatment for these soils is the same as that for the dunes of San Francisco: amending with lots of organic matter and mulch. My father, whose garden was in the foothills, used to haul in six or seven yards of turkey manure for his vegetable garden each and every year. Because the decomposed granite has lots of micronutrients but no nitrogen, potash or phosphorus, the addition of manure creates a perfect blend of

a coastal landscape

plant food and minerals that produces phenomenal results. Perfect drainage along with proper nutrients made my father's garden a winner.

All of the soils mentioned need to be amended and fertilized depending on location and past land use. Add organic matter such as compost, nitrogenated sawdust or good quality planting mix. Feed most plants, including lawns, during the growing season. Summer mulching is beneficial, as is planting native vegetation wherever possible.

A trip to any public garden in Northern California will give you many ideas for your own garden. A cutting garden like the one in Filoli can be yours on a smaller scale. Going through the wine country both in northern and central California will introduce you to many possible garden designs, formal and informal. You might discover that there are distinct Californian "English" gardens, which you can find in most of the coastal areas of California. Several gardens in Eureka, Fortuna, Fort Bragg and

red-hot poker

Mendocino are open to the public or are located in public places such as unique bed and breakfasts. Note the cool botanical gardens along the Sonoma and Mendocino coastal areas. Just over the hills from Jenner, you will be treated to cool redwood groves and, farther inland, golden fields of California poppies.

Phormium & fan palm (above) annual beds (below)

Whether you live in a downtown apartment or condo, the suburbs with a small lot or a ranch house with several acres of land, you can garden. Beautiful gardens are possible in all locations. This monthly guide should answer some of your specific questions about the wonderful gardening possibilities of Northern California. Use it to add your particular experiences for your own climate and garden. By keeping track of your gardening activities in this book, you can create your own custom-made gardening guide. It's been said that Thomas Jefferson wrote about his gardening successes in a daily gardening journal. We hope this book will inspire you as Jefferson's journal inspired him.

NORTHERN CALIFORNIA CLIMATE NORMALS 1931–2003

(Information adapted from the Western Regional Climate Center web site.)

ALTURAS

CATEGORY	JAN	FEB	MAR	APR	MAY	JUN	JUL	AUG	SEP	OCT	NOV	DEC	YEAR
DAILY MAXIMUM (°F)	41.6	45.8	51.9	59.9	68.2	77	87.5	86.8	79.1	66.9	51.9	43.6	63.4
DAILY MINIMUM (°F)	16.6	20.5	24.7	28.6	34.9	40.8	44.1	41.5	35.5	28.2	22.7	18	29.7
SNOWFALL (IN)	8.5	5.7	5.4	2.7	0.8	0.0	0.0	0.0	0.0	0.3	3.4	5.6	32.4
PRECIPITATION (IN)*	1.55	1.42	1.39	1.05	1.33	0.98	0.29	0.35	0.48	0.95	1.44	1.51	12.73

CRESCENT CITY

CATEGORY	JAN	FEB	MAR	APR	MAY	JUN	JUL	AUG	SEP	OCT	NOV	DEC	YEAR
DAILY MAXIMUM (°F)	54.8	55.8	56.3	58.2	60.9	63.6	65.3	66.2	66.6	63.6	58.3	55.3	60.4
DAILY MINIMUM (°F)	40.5	41.6	41.8	43.2	46.0	48.9	50.9	51.5	49.9	47.1	43.7	40.5	45.5
SNOWFALL (IN)	0.2	0.0	0.0	0.0	0.0	0.0	0.0	0.0	0.0	0.0	0.0	0.0	0.2
PRECIPITATION (IN)	11.67	8.96	8.43	4.51	3.20	1.38	0.38	0.76	1.68	5.16	9.13	10.80	66.06

EUREKA

CATEGORY	JAN	FEB	MAR	APR	MAY	JUN	JUL	AUG	SEP	OCT	NOV	DEC	YEAR
DAILY MAXIMUM (°F)	54.3	55.4	55.3	56.2	58.4	60.4	61.6	62.8	62.9	61.0	58.0	54.8	58.4
DAILY MINIMUM (°F)	41.5	42.8	43.0	44.6	47.8	50.6	52.3	53.1	51.5	48.4	45.0	41.8	46.9
SNOWFALL (IN)	0.1	0.1	0.0	0.0	0.0	0.0	0.0	0.0	0.0	0.0	0.0	0.1	0.3
PRECIPITATION (IN)	6.85	5.35	5.32	2.86	1.70	0.63	0.14	0.36	0.80	2.72	5.77	6.47	38.98

FRESNO

CATEGORY	JAN	FEB	MAR	APR	MAY	JUN	JUL	AUG	SEP	OCT	NOV	DEC	YEAR
DAILY MAXIMUM (°F)	54.3	61.5	66.8	74.7	83.2	91.5	98.0	96.1	90.4	79.9	65.3	54.5	76.3
DAILY MINIMUM (°F)	37.3	40.5	43.4	47.7	53.8	60.1	65.0	63.5	59.1	50.7	41.9	36.8	50.0
SNOWFALL (IN)	0.0	0.0	0.0	0.0	0.0	0.0	0.0	0.0	0.0	0.0	0.0	0.0	0.1
PRECIPITATION (IN)	2.18	1.94	1.95	0.99	0.35	0.16	0.01	0.02	0.19	0.52	1.18	1.50	10.98

REDDING

CATEGORY	JAN	FEB	MAR	APR	MAY	JUN	JUL	AUG	SEP	OCT	NOV	DEC	YEAR
DAILY MAXIMUM (°F)	54.9	59.7	65.2	72.5	81.7	90.2	98.4	96.4	90.7	78.7	64.6	55.7	75.7
DAILY MINIMUM (°F)	37.4	40.5	43.3	47.9	54.9	62.3	68.1	65.9	61.3	53.2	44.4	38.8	51.5
SNOWFALL (IN)	1.7	0.8	0.6	0.0	0.0	0.0	0.0	0.0	0.0	0.0	0.5	1.2	4.8
PRECIPITATION (IN)	7.96	5.89	5.00	2.99	1.48	0.97	0.16	0.31	0.78	2.19	4.69	6.95	39.37

SACRAMENTO

CATEGORY	JAN	FEB	MAR	APR	MAY	JUN	JUL	AUG	SEP	OCT	NOV	DEC	YEAR
DAILY MAXIMUM (°F)	53.2	59.5	64.6	71.0	77.9	85.6	91.4	90.3	86.0	76.6	64.0	53.9	72.8
DAILY MINIMUM (°F)	39.5	43.1	45.6	48.4	52.4	56.7	59.0	58.5	56.9	51.6	44.4	39.8	49.7
SNOWFALL (IN)	0.0	0.0	0.0	0.0	0.0	0.0	0.0	0.0	0.0	0.0	0.0	0.0	0.0
PRECIPITATION (IN)	3.73	3.22	2.66	1.40	0.61	0.16	0.01	0.03	0.31	0.93	2.01	3.07	18.14

*equivalent to rainfall

NORTHERN CALIFORNIA CLIMATE NORMALS 1931–2003

(Information adapted from the Western Regional Climate Center web site.)

CATEGORY	JAN	FEB	MAR	APR	MAY	JUN	JUL	AUG	SEP	OCT	NOV	DEC	YEAR	
DAILY MAXIMUM (°F)	57.4	59.6	60.2	60.9	61.2	62.6	63.4	64.4	66.2	66.1	62.2	57.5	61.8	SAN FRANCISCO
DAILY MINIMUM (°F)	43.9	45.9	46.5	47.4	49.5	51.4	53.4	54.5	54.4	52.2	48.1	44.3	49.3	
SNOWFALL (IN)	0.0	0.0	0.0	0.0	0.0	0.0	0.0	0.0	0.0	0.0	0.0	0.0	0.0	
PRECIPITATION (IN)	4.38	3.47	2.87	1.20	0.48	0.15	0.02	0.10	0.19	1.11	2.75	3.18	19.90	
DAILY MAXIMUM (°F)	57.9	62.0	65.3	69.9	74.3	79.2	82.1	81.8	80.7	74.6	65.1	58.0	70.9	SAN JOSE
DAILY MINIMUM (°F)	41.3	44.1	45.6	47.5	51.1	54.6	56.7	56.8	56.0	51.8	45.9	41.5	49.4	
SNOWFALL (IN)	0.0	0.0	0.0	0.0	0.0	0.0	0.0	0.0	0.0	0.0	0.0	0.0	0.0	
PRECIPITATION (IN)	3.06	2.49	2.31	1.06	0.40	0.09	0.04	0.09	0.21	0.73	1.73	2.28	14.49	
DAILY MAXIMUM (°F)	59.9	62.3	64.2	67.7	70.6	73.6	74.4	75.2	76.1	73.0	65.9	60.6	68.6	SANTA CRUZ
DAILY MINIMUM (°F)	39.1	41.1	42.0	43.4	46.5	49.4	51.7	51.9	50.9	47.3	42.7	39.1	45.4	
SNOWFALL (IN)	0.0	0.0	0.0	0.0	0.0	0.0	0.0	0.0	0.0	0.0	0.0	0.0	0.0	
PRECIPITATION (IN)	6.79	5.55	4.31	2.17	0.66	0.20	0.09	0.10	0.29	1.28	3.89	5.04	30.37	
DAILY MAXIMUM (°F)	55.0	58.4	62.3	68.7	77.4	86.5	95.0	93.8	87.8	77.1	63.7	55.9	73.5	SONORA
DAILY MINIMUM (°F)	33.1	34.9	37.7	41.6	46.7	52.3	58.1	57.1	52.6	45.0	37.4	33.2	44.2	
SNOWFALL (IN)	1.7	0.9	0.4	0.2	0.0	0.0	0.0	0.0	0.0	0.0	0.0	0.5	3.7	
PRECIPITATION (IN)	6.21	5.75	4.82	2.75	1.21	0.30	0.05	0.09	0.46	1.71	3.62	5.20	32.16	
DAILY MAXIMUM (°F)	53.3	60.5	65.6	73.0	80.7	88.3	94.1	92.6	88.0	78.3	64.3	53.6	74.4	STOCKTON
DAILY MINIMUM (°F)	37.6	40.6	42.6	46.2	51.6	57.0	60.6	60.1	57.2	50.3	42.2	37.2	48.6	
SNOWFALL (IN)	0.0	0.0	0.0	0.0	0.0	0.0	0.0	0.0	0.0	0.0	0.0	0.0	0.0	
PRECIPITATION (IN)	2.94	2.30	2.10	1.14	0.42	0.09	0.03	0.05	0.29	0.73	1.80	2.20	14.07	
DAILY MAXIMUM (°F)	38.5	40.3	43.8	50.6	59.5	68.5	77.7	77.2	69.8	58.8	46.6	40.4	56.0	TAHOE CITY
DAILY MINIMUM (°F)	18.9	20.0	22.7	26.9	32.7	38.6	44.1	43.7	39.0	32.3	25.6	21.0	30.5	
SNOWFALL (IN)	43.8	38.0	35.5	15.2	3.8	0.2	0.0	0.0	0.3	2.4	16.2	33.5	188.9	
PRECIPITATION (IN)	6.18	5.50	4.11	2.11	1.19	0.69	0.26	0.31	0.64	1.83	3.68	5.40	31.89	

NORTHERN CALIFORNIA CLIMATE EXTREMES 1931–2003

(Information adapted from the Western Regional Climate Center web site.)

ALTURAS

EXTREME HIGH (°F)   107.0 ON JULY 19, 1960

EXTREME LOW (°F)   -34.0 ON DECEMBER 9, 1972

EXTREME RAIN (IN)   10.00 ON FEBRUARY 6, 1937

EXTREME SNOW (IN)   33.5 IN JANUARY 1933

SAN FRANCISCO

EXTREME HIGH (°F)   99.0 ON OCTOBER 15, 1961

EXTREME LOW (°F)   26.0 ON DECEMBER 31, 1984

EXTREME RAIN (IN)   3.9 ON FEBRUARY 2, 1998

EXTREME SNOW (IN)   NO RECORDED SNOWFALL

CRESCENT CITY

EXTREME HIGH (°F)   93.0 ON JUNE 1, 1970

EXTREME LOW (°F)   19.0 ON DECEMBER 21, 1990

EXTREME RAIN (IN)   7.73 ON JANUARY 9, 1995

EXTREME SNOW (IN)   6.0 IN JANUARY, 1972

SAN JOSE

EXTREME HIGH (°F)   109.0 ON JUNE 14, 2000

EXTREME LOW (°F)   19.0 ON DECEMBER 22, 1990

EXTREME RAIN (IN)   3.6 ON JANUARY 30, 1968

EXTREME SNOW (IN)   0.5 IN FEBRUARY, 1976

EUREKA

EXTREME HIGH (°F)   87.0 ON OCTOBER 26, 1993

EXTREME LOW (°F)   21.0 ON DECEMBER 9, 1972

EXTREME RAIN (IN)   5.04 ON OCTOBER 29, 1950

EXTREME SNOW (IN)   3.5 IN FEBRUARY, 1989

SANTA CRUZ

EXTREME HIGH (°F)   107.0 ON SEPTEMBER 14, 1971

EXTREME LOW (°F)   19.0 ON DECEMBER 23, 1990

EXTREME RAIN (IN)   6.91 ON JANUARY 5, 1982

EXTREME SNOW (IN)   NO RECORDED SNOWFALL

FRESNO

EXTREME HIGH (°F)   112.0 ON JULY 5, 1991

EXTREME LOW (°F)   18.0 ON JANUARY 10, 1949

EXTREME RAIN (IN)   2.21 ON JANUARY 25, 1969

EXTREME SNOW (IN)   2.2 IN JANUARY, 1962

SONORA

EXTREME HIGH (°F)   113.0 ON JUNE 22, 1961

EXTREME LOW (°F)   8.0 ON DECEMBER 9, 1972

EXTREME RAIN (IN)   7.1 ON DECEMBER 27, 1955

EXTREME SNOW (IN)   30.5 IN JANUARY, 1933

REDDING

EXTREME HIGH (°F)   118.0 ON AUGUST 10, 1971

EXTREME LOW (°F)   17.0 ON JANUARY 20, 1937

EXTREME RAIN (IN)   7.3 ON DECEMBER 22, 1964

EXTREME SNOW (IN)   29.0 IN JANUARY, 1950

STOCKTON

EXTREME HIGH (°F)   114.0 ON JULY 14, 1972

EXTREME LOW (°F)   16.0 ON JANUARY 11, 1949

EXTREME RAIN (IN)   3.01 ON JANUARY 21, 1967

EXTREME SNOW (IN)   0.3 IN FEBRUARY, 1976

SACRAMENTO

EXTREME HIGH (°F)   114.0 ON JULY 17, 1925

EXTREME LOW (°F)   17.0 ON DECEMBER 11, 1932

EXTREME RAIN (IN)   28.0 ON APRIL 20, 1880

EXTREME SNOW (IN)   NO RECORDED SNOWFALL

TAHOE CITY

EXTREME HIGH (°F)   94.0 ON AUGUST 15, 1933

EXTREME LOW (°F)   -16.0 ON DECEMBER 11, 1972

EXTREME RAIN (IN)   6.77 ON DECEMBER 23, 1964

EXTREME SNOW (IN)   195.5 IN JANUARY, 1952

AVERAGE NUMBER OF CLEAR DAYS

This data is based on daylight hours only. A clear day has 0%–30% average sky cover;
a partly cloudy day 40%–70% cloud cover; a cloudy day 80%–100% cloud cover.

	JAN	FEB	MAR	APR	MAY	JUN	JUL	AUG	SEP	OCT	NOV	DEC	YEAR
BISHOP	11	11	13	14	15	20	22	23	23	20	15	14	201
BLUE CANYON	9	8	9	10	12	18	26	25	22	17	10	9	174
EUREKA	6	5	6	6	6	7	7	6	9	8	6	6	78
FRESNO	5	8	11	14	18	23	27	26	24	20	12	7	194
MT SHASTA CITY	9	8	8	10	12	16	25	24	21	14	9	7	164
OAKLAND	9	8	10	11	12	15	17	15	16	14	11	9	147
REDDING	8	8	8	8	11	17	25	25	22	18	11	10	172
RED BLUFF	8	8	9	11	15	19	27	25	23	16	10	7	178
SACRAMENTO	7	8	10	12	17	22	27	26	24	19	10	8	188
SAN FRANCISCO AP	9	8	10	11	14	16	21	19	18	16	11	9	160
STOCKTON	5	7	10	12	17	22	27	26	23	19	9	7	184

HARDINESS ZONES

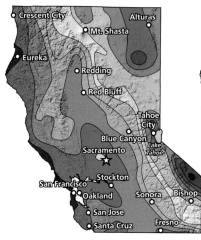

Average Annual Minimum Temperature

Zone	Temp (°F)	Zone	Temp (°F)
	-20 to -25	**7b**	10 to 5
5a	-15 to -20	**8a**	15 to 10
5b	-10 to -15	**8b**	20 to 15
6a	-5 to -10	**9a**	25 to 20
6b	0 to -5	**9b**	30 to 25
7a	5 to 0	**10a**	35 to 30

ANNUAL PRECIPITATION

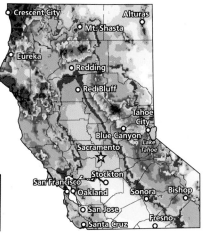

Inches per Year

0 - 5		45 - 50	
5 - 10		50 - 55	
10 - 15		55 - 60	
15 - 20		60 - 65	
20 - 25		65 - 70	
25 - 30		70 - 75	
30 - 35		75 - 80	
35 - 40		80 - 100	
40 - 45		over 100	

JANUARY

*Now is the time to plan
and plant the garden that will
blossom come spring.*

JANUARY

1

Happy New Gardening Year!

2

It is time to check out your gardening tools.

3

Don't forget to get the blades of that lawnmower sharpened.

4

5

6

7

'Olympiad' (*left*) was introduced in 1984 and named for the Los Angeles Olympics of that same year. This fine hybrid tea rose works well as part of a mixed border or as a specimen. Its thick petals are not harmed by rain, and the flowers maintain their color from the time they open until their petals fall. Camellia in bloom (*right*)

Most gardens have had adequate water, but look out for areas under the eaves of houses where winter moisture hasn't reached. These plants should be watered just to keep the ground moist. If you planted Iceland poppies and other winter-blooming flowers, make sure you clean them up between rainstorms. Now is a good time to visit your local nurseries to see what is in bloom to offset those after-Christmas blahs. If you expect a light frost, spray foliage of frost-sensitive plants with water in the evening to keep them from frost damage.

Don't forget to top up your bird-feeders regularly. Feeding the birds encourages them to keep visiting in summer when they will help keep your insect pest populations under control.

THINGS TO DO

Clean the foliage of your houseplants. When light levels are low, it is important for plants to be able to use whatever light is available. As a bonus, you might help reduce insect populations because their eggs will likely be wiped off along with the dust.

Order gardening and seed catalogs to look through even if you don't start your own seeds. Choose and order seeds early for the best selection and for early starting. Sort through the seeds you have, test them for viability (see p.17) and throw out any that don't germinate or that you won't grow. Trade seeds with gardening friends.

Place extra seeds in a sealed paper envelope and keep them in the refrigerator. They will last for several years this way.

8

9

*Check your garden shops for bareroot roses,
fruit trees and berry bushes.
Blueberries, artichokes, strawberries,
raspberries and many other small fruits
are available in local nurseries.*

10

11

*Check houseplants to make sure
the soil isn't saturated, and keep them away
from hot or cold drafts.*

12

13

14

Camellia (*left*), primroses and Iceland poppies (*right*)
are reliable January bloomers.

Cut the branches of your spring-flowering shrubs to force blooms indoors.

Many summer- and fall-flowering trees, shrubs and perennials can be pruned this month, but don't prune plants that flower on old wood.

Start perennial seeds indoors for spring planting. Seed-starting tips are listed in February (see p. 33).

Dormant trees, shrubs, vines and perennials can be planted, but avoid working with the soil when it is very wet because you can damage its structure.

To control insects and diseases, use lime-sulphur on most trees and roses and liquid copper spray on apricots and peaches. Combine horticultural oil with both sprays to increase their effectiveness.

Primroses, pansies, cineraria, Iceland poppies and violas can be planted now. Dwarf cyclamen and Julian primroses will give you shots of instant color and look terrific in small flowerbeds, moss baskets and strawberry pots.

Bareroot roses and blueberries are available this month, as are deciduous fruit trees and kiwi vines in containers. Plant garlic, onions and potatoes now for harvest in late summer.

High mountain gardeners will want to watch for snow damage to trees and shrubs. Gently knock heavy snow off branches, but leave any ice that forms to melt naturally.

To test older seeds for viability, place 10 seeds between two layers of moist paper towel and put them in a sealed container. Keep the paper evenly dampened but not too wet. Seeds may rot if the paper towel is too moist. Check each day to see if the seeds have sprouted. If less than half the seeds sprout, buy new ones.

15

16

Check houseplants regularly for common indoor insect pests such as whiteflies, spider mites and mealybugs.

17

18

January is a good time of year to finish the garden clean up. Check your fertilizers and garden chemicals for dates and labels. Contact your local agriculture department for the location of disposal sites in your area.

19

20

You can find kerria (*left*) in your nursery in full bloom for a dash of yellow cheer in the garden. Other interesting plants you might consider for your garden are (*opposite page, clockwise from top*) full moon maple, viburnum and Japanese maple.

Plants that add variety to a winter garden:

- Arborvitae (*Thuja spp.*), False Cypress (*Chamaecyparis spp.*) or Juniper (*Juniperus spp.*): evergreen branches
- Clematis (*Clematis spp.*): fuzzy seedheads
- Corkscrew Hazel (*Corylus spp.*): twisted and contorted branches
- Cotoneaster (*Cotoneaster spp.*): persistent red berries
- Dogwoods (*Cornus spp.*): red, purple or yellow stems
- Highbush Cranberry (*Viburnum trilobum*): bright red berries
- Kerria (*Kerria japonica*): bright green stems
- Maples (*Acer ginnala, Acer palmatum*): attractive bark and branching patterns
- Shrub Roses (*Rosa spp.*): brightly colored hips
- Winged Euonymus (*Euonymus alatus*): corky ridges on the branches
- Autumn Flowering Cherry (*Prunus subhirtella autumnalis*): blooms in fall and again in early spring

GARDEN DESIGN

January is a great time for garden planning. In winter, the bones of the garden are laid bare, so you can take a good look at the garden's overall structure.

Imagine the garden you'd like to have, and keep a notebook and your diagrams handy so you can jot down ideas as they come to you.

As you look out your windows at the winter landscape, think about what could make your garden look more attractive in winter. Features such as birdbaths, ponds, benches, decks and winding pathways of stone, gravel or bricks enhance the look and function of your garden year-round. Persistent fruit, unusual bark and branch patterns, evergreens and colorfully stemmed shrubs also provide winter interest.

JANUARY

This is a good time to start putting out snail bait. Sluggo™ is an effective mollusk eliminator and is safe to use around pets and birds.

Nurseries are beginning to bring in tomato plants, but don't plant them in the ground until after Easter.

Dogwood (*left*) provides winter interest, making it a good foundation plant for garden beds in winter, when most perennials are not at their best. *Opposite page:* examples of topiary, mini topiary at Filoli and bonsai

PRUNING TIPS

At this time of year, as your coniferous plants have finished their spring growth, you can shape them into patterns to fit your own garden style. With judicious pruning, you can often extend the usefulness of conifers in your landscape. Illustrated are a few of the patterns you might wish to have in your own garden. If some of these styles appeal to you, your local nurseries will have some of these plants already shaped and ready to be planted. Keep in mind that pruning plants like the ones pictured may require a professional arborist. Once they have been shaped, it is up to you to keep them that way.

- Prune at the right time of year. Prune deciduous fruit trees, shade trees, roses and shrubs now. Acid-loving plants, such as azaleas, camellias and rhododendrons, are best pruned while they are in bloom or immediately thereafter.

- Use the correct tool for the size of branch to be removed: hand pruners for growth up to $3/4$" in diameter; long-handled loppers for growth up to $1^1/2$" in diameter; or a pruning saw for growth up to 6" in diameter.

Don't prune trees or shrubs when growth has started and buds are swelling. Prune before growth starts in spring or wait until plants have leafed out.

28

29

30

31

*If you haven't sprayed your roses
and fruit trees with lime-sulfur and oil,
now is the time to do so. Apricots should be
sprayed with liquid copper.*

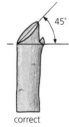

45°

correct

too low

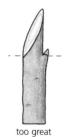

too great

too high

Pruning angles

thinning cuts

Thin trees and shrubs to promote the growth of younger,
healthier branches. Doing so rejuvenates a plant.

- Always use clean, sharp tools.

- Always use hand pruners or loppers with the blade side towards the plant and the hook towards the part to be removed.

When pruning, avoid the following:

- Don't leave stubs. Whether you are cutting off a large branch or deadheading a small shrub, always cut back to a bud. Branches should be removed to the branch collar, and smaller growth should be cut back to a bud or branch union. There is no absolute set angle for pruning, but generally a 45° angle is preferable. Each plant should be pruned according to its individual needs.

- Never use pruning paint or paste. Trees have a natural ability to create a barrier between living and dead wood. Painting over a cut impairs this ability.

- Avoid topping any of your trees. Topping weakens trees, shortens their lives and looks ugly.

Many plants need extensive pruning because they are planted in the wrong place. Keep in mind that the little one-gallon plant you buy today will grow, possibly into something much larger than you have room for, so you should know its mature size before planting.

Most indoor plants will benefit from a flushing of their root systems. Take them to the sink or bathtub and water three or four times, let them drain and place in a tray filled with stones or marbles to prevent root rot. About 95% of houseplants die from standing in trays filled with water.

FEBRUARY

*The longer days and spells of warm weather
turn our thoughts to the
upcoming gardening season.*

FEBRUARY

1

2

This month will be your last chance to prune and spray dormant oil on deciduous trees and shrubs. Follow the directions carefully to avoid harming beneficial insects.

3

4

Small fruit plants are at their prime in most nurseries now. Strawberries, blueberries and raspberries should head your list.

5

6

7

Crabapple blossoms (*left and far right*); there's still time for bareroot plantings of fruit trees this month. Sunny yellow acacia blooms (*near right*) are fragrant and attract birds, bees and other creatures to your garden.

Groundhog Day reminds us that there may be more wet weather coming. Don't be fooled by those false springs that make us want to plant those hot weather vegetables and flowers. Wait until March to get excited. If you haven't fed your citrus trees, now is a good time to get started. Pruning and dormant spraying are still the main gardening tasks for this month.

THINGS TO DO

February is a great month for making preparations that will keep things moving smoothly once the season kicks into high gear. Finish up any pruning you haven't done so far. Roses are starting to sprout, and though you can still prune them, don't wait too much longer. If fruit trees are starting to bloom, you can still prune because they remain dormant until the leaves start sprouting. Spraying roses now with a strong solution of lime-sulfur will prevent diseases from getting an early start. Feeding your roses alfalfa pellets will improve their response to rose fertilizer come March. This is the preferable time to repot all of your outside plants, including small trees and shrubs. Now is also a good time to order bareroot fruit trees, send in seed catalog orders and clean and repair garden tools.

You can cut branches off your blooming deciduous plants and bring them into the house for colorful accents to remind you that spring is coming.

8

9

All your outdoor duties will take your attention away from your houseplants, so check them now for insects.

10

11

Danger of frost still exists everywhere but on the coast. If you're going to start seeds, now is the time to do it. You can get a head start on the weeds by preparing all of your vegetable and flower beds at this time.

12

13

14

Mexican sunflower (*left*) does well in sunny coastal climates as well as hot interior valleys. *Opposite page, clockwise from top:* coreopsis, hollyhock, spider flower (*cleome*)

The general rule for starting any seed is the smaller the seed, the more difficult it is to start. Many people opt to start their own tomato plants. Here is a list of easier seeds to start:

- Baby's Breath (*Gypsophila elegans*)
- Bachelor's Button (*Centaurea cyanus*)
- Coreopsis (*Coreopsis* species)
- Forget-Me-Not (*Anchusa capensis*)
- Hollyhock (*Alcea* species)
- Lobelia (*Lobelia erinus*)
- Mexican Sunflower (*Tithonia rotundifolia*)
- Spider Flower (*Cleome spinosa*)
- Statice (*Limonium sinuatum*)

Most soils in California have a pH of 6.5 and higher. Periodically check the pH of your garden soil with a small kit that can be purchased from local nurseries. Alfalfa meal or pellets can be added to most soils, including lawns, to balance the pH and add important trace elements to the soil. If the pH is around 7.5, the alfalfa will correct this situation. A pH reading higher than 7.5 will necessitate adding soil sulfur or aluminum sulfate.

FEBRUARY

15

16

If you haven't already done so, clean up all of last year's growth on your perennials. Plants such as daylilies will benefit from such a clean up. Mexican sage can be cut back along with your herb patch.

17

18

This is the last call for planting any bareroot material. If your space is limited, plant three semi-dwarf fruit trees in the same hole.

19

20

21

Flowering quince (*left*) blooms early in the month, taking the gloom of winter away. Blooming in February (*opposite page, clockwise from top left*): abutilon, magnolia, pansy

Slugs and snails are always a potential problem in Northern California. Hand-picking takes courage, but will do the job. Unless you enjoy slime on your fingers, you will need a flashlight and gloves.

If you are really in a hurry to dress up the garden, 4" pots of color are on the market for a quick fix. Calendula, pansies, primroses, snapdragons, candytuft and Iceland poppies will jazz up the garden until the hot weather hits in June.

If we hit a dry spell, make sure you water all of your trees and shrubs, particularly frost-sensitive plants.

During warm spells, high mountain gardeners should prune damaged limbs off trees and do a general inspection of the garden to make sure nothing has begun to sprout prematurely.

As the days start to lengthen, indoor plants may start to show signs of new growth. Increase watering and apply a weak fertilizer (1/4 strength) only after they begin to grow.

Seedlings will be weak and floppy if they don't get enough light. Consider purchasing a fluorescent or other grow light *(below)* to provide extra illumination for them.

FEBRUARY

Camellias are in full bloom now, and it is
important to keep the old blooms cleaned up.
Blossom blight can be a problem next fall
if the blooms are allowed to stay.

If you have problems with your seedlings
damping off, grind up peat moss and
sprinkle it lightly over the top of the plants.
Make sure seedlings have plenty
of air circulation.

Pick 'Voodoo' *(left)* if you want a
vibrant orange-pink hybrid tea to add
some sizzle to your garden. 'Voodoo'
grows to 4–6' and resists disease
well. It blooms best late in the
season, and looks especially good
when mass planted. *Opposite page:* seed-
starting supplies

STARTING SEEDS

What you need for starting seeds:
- containers such as pots, trays or peat pots
- seed-starting mix
- plastic bags or tray covers
- water mister and heating coil (optional)

Tips for starting seeds:
- Moisten the soil before you fill the containers.
- Firm the soil down, but don't pack it too tightly.
- Don't cover seeds that need light to germinate.
- Plant large seeds individually by poking a hole in the soil with the tip of a pen or pencil and then dropping the seed in the hole.
- Spread small seeds evenly across the soil surface, then lightly cover with more soil.
- To spread small seeds, place them in the crease of a folded piece of paper and gently tap the bottom of the fold to roll them onto the soil.
- Mix very tiny seeds with very fine sand before planting to spread them out more evenly.
- Plant only one type of seed in each container. Some seeds will germinate before others, and it is difficult to keep both seeds and seedlings happy in the same container.
- Cover pots or trays of seeds with clear plastic bags or tray covers to keep them moist.
- Seeds do not need bright, direct light to germinate and can be kept in an out-of-the-way place until they begin to sprout.

Tips for growing healthy seedlings:
- To prevent crowding, transplant seedlings to individual containers once they have three or four true leaves.
- Space plants so that the leaves do not overshadow those of neighboring plants.
- Don't fertilize young seedlings until the first true leaves appear. Then water with a weak fertilizer once a week.
- Keep seedlings in bright light to reduce stretching.
- Once the seeds germinate, remove the plastic cover and continue to keep in a bright area.

To prevent seedlings from damping off, always use a sterile soil mix, thoroughly clean containers before using them, maintain good air circulation around seedlings and keep the soil moist, not soggy.

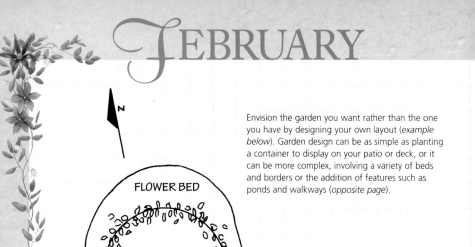

FEBRUARY

Envision the garden you want rather than the one you have by designing your own layout (*example below*). Garden design can be as simple as planting a container to display on your patio or deck, or it can be more complex, involving a variety of beds and borders or the addition of features such as ponds and walkways (*opposite page*).

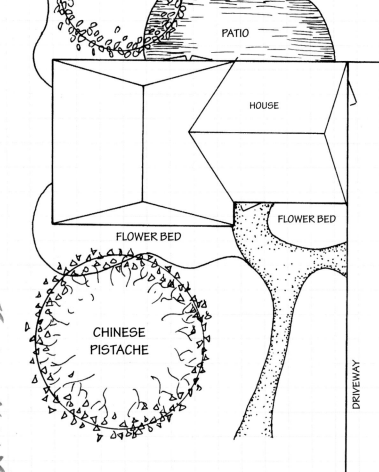

N

FLOWER BED

HAWTHORN

PATIO

HOUSE

FLOWER BED

FLOWER BED

CHINESE
PISTACHE

DRIVEWAY

Now is the best time of year to use horticultural oil or dormant oil on all of your evergreen trees and shrubs. Doing so will eliminate most of the eggs on junipers and other evergreen shrubs. Dormant oil takes the color off blue evergreens such as blue spruce, so check for mites first before spraying because it may not be necessary.

MARCH

Spring is in full swing in all areas except the snow-bound Sierras. The rains will slow down and the major storms are in the past.

MARCH

1

2

As the weather warms, you can put seedlings outside during the day to harden them for their eventual re-location in the garden. Don't leave them out overnight at this time.

3

4

Once your Cymbidium orchid's blooms start to fade, you can divide the plant.

5

6

7

If you have acidic soil, consider an azalea, such as this Exbury Hybrid (*left*), for vibrant color in early March. Prune flowering dogwoods (*top right*) after they have bloomed. California lilac with camellia (*bottom right*)

Warm spells allow us to start enjoying the outside. Usually a fine break in the weather gives us a chance to turn the soil and prepare beds for planting. There can still be a late frost, but normally you can start planting most vegetables except for cold-sensitive plants such as tomatoes and peppers. Most plants in nurseries have been hardened off sufficiently to take any dip in the temperature. Now is also the time to plant summer bulbs such as amaryllis, callas, gladiolus, lilies and tuberous begonias. For gardeners in the Sierra mountains, starting vegetable seeds indoors this month for planting later in spring will make the most of a short growing season.

THINGS TO DO

If you haven't started feeding your roses, start feeding them now with your favorite rose food once a month. Camellias, azaleas and other acid-loving plants should be fed monthly until September. Watch for aphids on these plants because bugs love the new, tender growth. Spraying plants with water from your garden hose a couple of times a week will keep aphids under control.

8

9

Start feeding your lawn. Use an organic fertilizer, and you won't have to do the job more than once every six weeks. If you must use a weed killer, spot spray to minimize the amount of chemical used.

10

11

Watch out for tent caterpillars this month. Spray with Bt (Bacillus thuringiensis) if they are around your favorite oak tree. Large trees may have to be professionally sprayed, but make sure they use Bt and not dangerous chemicals.

12

13

14

Some of the first blossoms you see as winter loses its punch are the pink blooms of bergenia (*left*). The tropical foliage accents established landscapes and can be a delightful groundcover under trees. Spirea (*far right*); hardy kiwi (*near right*); 'Annabelle' hydrangea (*bottom right*)

Winter rains have kept us from controlling the weeds in the garden, and that can be a hassle when we start to remove them. Resist the temptation to rototill them under, however. Instead, pull out as many as you can by hand prior to tilling because tall weeds will choke up your machine.

These unusual plants are worth trying in your garden:

- False Spirea (*Sorbaria sorbifolia*)
- Hardy Kiwi (*Actinidia arguta*)
- Hydrangea (*Hydrangea*), all varieties
- Japanese Spirea (*Spirea japonica*)
- Potentilla (*Potentilla* spp.)
- Red-twig Dogwood (*Cornus alba*)
- Yellow or Purple-leafed Elders (*Sambucus*)

MARCH

15

16

As the weather warms up and settles down, you may plant the seedlings you started earlier. Wait a couple of weeks before planting cold-sensitive tomatoes and peppers.

17

18

If you haven't done so, it is time to feed your perennials and prepare the beds for annuals.

19

20

Start cleaning up old blooms from your spring-blooming bulbs. Removing seedpods from daffodils will increase their energy for next year's blooming cycle.

21

Tulip (*left*); if planted early enough in fall, clematis (*top right*) flowers the first summer; daffodils in bloom (*far right*); tulips and hostas in a gorgeous spring-blooming bed (*bottom right*).

Before doing any digging, call your utility companies to locate any buried wires, cables or pipes to prevent injury and save time and money.

Keep off your lawn when it is very wet to avoid damaging the grass or compacting the soil.

If a plant needs well-drained soil and full sun to thrive, it will be healthiest and best able to fight off problems in those conditions. Work with your plants' natural tendencies.

MARCH

22

23

*Clean out your birdfeeders
and replace old seed.*

24

25

*Before planting any bedding plant,
make sure to loosen the roots to prevent
the plant from becoming root bound.*

26

27

28

Rhododendrons (*left*) grow well and look good when
planted in groups. They thrive in sheltered locations
and require fertile, acidic, moist and well-
drained soil to do well. Rhododendron
'Irene Kostner' in combination
with *scilla* (*top right*); flowering
quince (*bottom right*)

Apply aged compost to established trees and shrubs and cultivate into the soil.

At this time of year, adding grass clippings to your compost pile will heat it up and make it decay more rapidly. If coarse material isn't decomposing, you may not have cut it up sufficiently. Next fall when you rake up tree leaves and prunings, grind leaves by putting them on your driveway and running your lawn mower over them. Larger debris can damage your mower, so cut up branches by hand or with a woodchipper.

Check the new growth of your hostas and other perennials that go dormant to make sure the snails, slugs and earwigs are not attacking the new shoots. Frosts in many areas are now over, and you are safe in pruning frost-sensitive plants such as hibiscus and bougainvillea.

Harden annuals and perennials off before planting them by gradually exposing them to longer periods of time outside on a porch or deck. Doing so gives your plants time to adapt to outdoor weather conditions and reduces the chance of transplant shock.

Remove only damaged branches when planting trees or shrubs, and leave the plant to settle in for at least one year before you begin any formative pruning. Plants need all the branches and leaves they have when they are trying to get established.

Keep an eye out for garden shows in your area. They all are worth a visit.

Don't plant vigorous spreaders in rock gardens with tiny alpine plants or large shrubs right next to walkways.

MARCH

The single most important thing you can do when planting is to make sure you have the right plant in the right location. Consider the mature size of the plant and its cultural requirements.

The charming shrub rose 'Graham Thomas' (*below*) resembles an old English rose. It bears beautiful buttery yellow blooms on long, arching stems. In cooler climates, its narrow, upright growth habit makes it useful as a shrub; in warmer climates, it can be trained to climb walls, fences or tall pillars.

PLANTING TIPS

Early spring is prime planting season for trees, shrubs, vines and perennials. They often establish more quickly when they are planted just as they are about to break dormancy. They are full of growth hormones, and they recover quickly from transplant shock.

A few things to keep in mind when planting your garden:

- Never work with your soil when it is very wet or very dry.
- Avoid planting during the hottest, sunniest part of the day. Choose an overcast day, or plant in the early morning or late afternoon.
- Prepare your soil before you plant to avoid damaging roots later.
- Get your new plants into the ground as soon as possible when you get them home. Roots can get hot and dry out quickly in containers. Keep plants in a shady spot if you must wait to plant them.
- Most plants are happiest when planted at the same depth they have always grown at. Trees in particular can be killed by too deep a planting.
- Plants should be well watered when they are newly planted. Watering deeply and infrequently will encourage the strongest root growth.
- Check the root zone before watering. The soil surface may appear dry when the roots are still moist.
- Fall is also a great time to plant in Northern California, and the above tips are true for that season as well.

Trees less than 5' tall do not need staking unless they are in a very windy location. Unstaked trees develop stronger root systems and trunks.

staking a tree properly

planting a balled-and-burlapped tree

planting a bareroot tree

APRIL

Spring is here at last—time to take advantage of all of the new flowers that are in your local nurseries.

APRIL

1

2

You are going to be visited by a foamy mass
on some of your plants. It is spittlebug.
Just wash it off.

3

4

Some of your winter-blooming flowers
should be replaced with summer annuals.

5

6

7

The columbine (*left*) is a beautiful flower that some
say resembles a bird in flight. Its jewel-like colors
herald the coming of summer. *Opposite page,
clockwise from top:* English daisies,
foxgloves, marigolds

We are most attracted to plants that are in full bloom. To avoid having a one-season garden, visit your garden center regularly over the spring, summer and fall. Plants that are flowering at different times will catch your eye and give you a chance to fill your garden with a diverse selection of plants.

In frost-free areas, all garden planting is finally off and running this month. Soil preparation will start paying off in your vegetable garden as you plant tomatoes, peppers, basil, corn, squash and other plants. Keep your lawn fed for best performance. It will respond to a feeding of liquid fertilizer such as fish emulsion and VF 11. Color up the dead-looking spots with your favorite annuals. English daisies, marigold, petunias, lobelia, alyssum, cosmos, wax-leafed begonias, salvia and other summer-flowering plants are now available in flats and 4" pots.

APRIL

8

9

Don't forget to check your houseplants for insects. They will have awakened with the spring.

10

11

Coastal gardeners can still plant cool-weather vegetable crops such as spinach, cabbage and broccoli.

12

13

14

Consider planting daylilies (*left and top right*) this spring. Though each bloom lasts only a day, these lilies are easygoing, prolific and versatile, and come in an almost infinite variety of forms, sizes and colors; *arabis* and New Guinea hybrid impatiens (*bottom left*); Busy Lizzie impatiens, *I. walleriana* (*bottom right*)

THINGS TO DO

Now is the time of year to clean up your flowering shrubs such as azaleas and rhododendrons. Don't be afraid to shear back your azaleas to keep them compact and encourage more flowers for next year. Acid-loving plants need monthly feeding of acid plant food from now until the middle of September. Take cuttings for new plants from your azaleas as well as carnations, chrysanthemums, geraniums and succulents.

If you go shopping for plants and can't plant them right away, place them in a shady area where you won't forget to water them. In all cases, don't let them go unplanted for longer than one week.

Check your citrus trees for sucker growth. Large, spiky growth coming from below the graft is a problem and should be eliminated. Citruses need feeding once a month all year long.

Seeds sown directly into the garden may take longer to germinate than those planted indoors, but the resulting plants will be stronger.

15

16

Bougainvillea, tropical hibiscus and other tropical plants are available in nurseries. Note that they will need special treatment come winter.

17

18

If you are looking for new plants for your garden, visit your local nurseries for ideas. Perennials are especially important at this time.

19

20

21

Cosmos (*left*). *Opposite page, clockwise from top left:* begonias, gladiola, sage and peppers can be planted before the last spring frost

Many plants prefer to grow in warm weather. Sow these seeds directly into the soil this month:

- Corn (*Zea mays*)
- Cosmos (*Cosmos* spp.)
- Dwarf Bedding Dahlias (*Dahlia* spp.)
- Fuchsias (*Fuchsia* spp.)
- Gladiolas (*Gladiolus* spp.)
- Peppers (*Capiscum annuum*)
- Sages (*Salvia* spp.)
- String Beans (*Phaseolus vulgaris*)
- Sweet Alyssum (*Lobularia maritima*)
- Tomatoes (*Lycopersicon escalentum*)
- Wax-leafed Begonias (*Begonia semperflorens*)
- Zucchini (*Cucurbita pepo*)

22

23

When planting, make sure you allow for the ultimate growth of the plant.

24

25

To get rid of those pesky weeds in your brick and sidewalks, try white vinegar sprayed on a warm day. Most weeds are killed with one application.

26

27

28

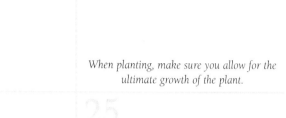

You can depend on aubrieta (*left*) to put on a great floral show in spring. *Opposite page, clockwise from top:* bearded iris; espaliered apple tree; strawberry

You might look into the possibility of growing your own cutting garden. Certain marigolds (X15 and X20 series) have large blooms and wonderfully fragrant flowers. A visit to your rose garden can add to any bouquet, and Dutch iris can be a wonderful addition to any flower arrangement for the home.

Your fruit trees need special attention at this time of year. If they have finished flowering, you can thin out the clusters of fruit on apples, apricots and peaches to make the fruit larger. Leave two or three of the best-formed fruit on each cluster. A healthy application of chicken manure watered in will see the tree through the season until fall without further care. If peach leaf curl has attacked your tree, just fertilize it now and keep the distorted leaves raked up.

Now with the rains no longer doing our irrigation, it is time to check your watering system for cracks or leaks. Flush out drip irrigation systems and check the emitters for stray overwintering insects such as earwigs. Make sure the timers on your automatic sprinklers are in good shape. Use this gardening guide to note your watering schedule.

Apply a 3" mulch (*left*) around plants now to protect roots from the hot, dry weather to come. Cover just the roots and leave the area around the stems bare to prevent crown rot.

Lilies are long-lived, easy-to-grow perennials. They look superb in floral arrangements combined with flowers such as baby's breath (*below*).

Opposite page, clockwise from top left: double columbine 'Nora Barlow'; *Salvia*, snapdragon and lamb's ears among others in a mixed bed; native plants in a xeriscape planting

Gardeners in the Sierra mountains may be able to sow wildflower seeds this month in a sunny, moist location, weather permitting. Try some California columbines or Sierra lupines, usually good flowers for mountain areas. Now is also a good time to start seeds for annuals and vegetables in a sunny location indoors for planting later in spring when the weather warms up. Mountain gardeners can also begin to prune deciduous trees this month before any new growth appears.

PROBLEM AREAS IN THE GARDEN

Keep track of these potential problem areas in your garden.

- If coastal winds have been a problem this winter, plant a hedge this spring for better wind protection.
- If some of your frost-sensitive plants have been damaged, don't prune until the danger of frost is over.
- Check for standing water around trees and shrubs this time of year. If you have had treewells around them, they need to be moved before more rain floods the area again.
- Hillside erosion should be noted and corrected this spring after rain has ceased. If it is a major job, call in a soils engineer for a consultation. The cost will be well worth it.

MAY

May is one of the most wonderful months to enjoy not only Mother's Day, but the fruits of your labors in the garden as well.

MAY

1

2

All stops are out in your flowerbeds and vegetable gardens. You have to visit your local nurseries almost weekly to keep up with all the new plant materials available.

3

4

With hot weather coming very soon, remember to mulch around all of your trees and shrubs. Not only does this conserve water, but it protects plants from the scorching days to come.

5

6

7

The Japanese anemone or windflower (*left*) is an attractive plant at all stages. Some species bloom in spring while others reserve their lovely displays for fall.

May is truly the best weather month in Northern California. You not only have the water reservoirs filling up from the Sierra snowmelt, but the air is clean and the climate is perfect for spending time in the garden. Mowing lawns, weeding and other garden chores still call us, but you can attack all of these with a smile as you see the blooms of the garden chase any winter blues away.

THINGS TO DO

The new gardening season is upon us big time, so start plotting to eliminate dull spots in your perennial beds. Although you can give the garden a quick fix using annuals from local nurseries, with planning you can also have a perennial garden that won't require an annual fix. Cut off any seedpods or ugly growth from the garden, and put all of that stuff in your compost along with any lawn clippings. If you haven't done so, plant your vegetable garden using lots of chicken manure, compost and alfalfa meal or pellets to enrich your soil. All vegetables and flowers can be planted this month.

Start mulching around your trees, shrubs and ground covers. Except for the Central Valley, we have very few days over 100°F. When we do get these few hot days, plants suffer. The heat damage can be minimized by mulching or spraying foliage with an anti-desiccant.

Clean up all of the blooms on your saucer magnolia (*top right*) once it stops blooming. Descanso varieties of lilacs (*bottom right*) do well in the warm areas of our region because they do not need the winter cold to bloom. Remember to clean off spent blooms once a year.

8

9

All gardens will benefit from a side feeding of manure or compost tea or other type of liquid fertilizer.

10

11

Pay close attention to tuberous begonias and fuchsias—they will need weekly feeding if they are in containers or hanging baskets. Fish emulsion and VF 11 work wonders.

12

13

14

Clematis such as C. 'Gravetye Beauty' (*left*) is a popular perennial vine with beautiful, showy flowers in many shapes and sizes. By planting several varieties, you can have clematis in bloom from spring to fall. *Opposite page, clockwise from top: Clematis* 'Hagley Hybrid'; *Clematis* 'Etoile Violette'

Spring has come at last to the high mountains as many of the wildflowers announce the wonders of the fields that have lain under snow since October. Vegetable gardening can begin in earnest but is limited to plants that are hardy to cold weather. Cabbage, Brussels sprouts, broccoli, spinach, carrots, beets, short-season zucchini, string beans, lima beans, lettuce of every kind, Swiss chard and arugula will give you all you can eat even after the first frosts in September or October. Those with a sense of adventure can try tomatoes, but choose those varieties that ripen in short periods of time. Consult your seed catalogs for the shortest day varieties. Lemon cucumbers will give you a bountiful harvest before the first freeze. Row covers will help extend your season and protect plants from insects and four-legged animals such as deer and rabbits. All types of onions are a good bet for these areas.

Cymbidium orchids (*center right*) can be divided after they have finished blooming. The flowering stem on your moth orchid (*Phalaenopsis*) should never be cut off (*right*). It will rebloom from this stem in about six weeks.

15

16

You should check for insect damage on all of your trees and shrubs at this time of year. If you see damage, contact your local nursery or county Agricultural Commissioner.

17

18

Spring-flowering plants can be pruned now to force new growth for flowers next spring.

19

20

21

Dianthus (*left*); *opposite page, clockwise from top:* a healthy lawn with impatiens border in a shady location; xeriscaping in front garden for sunny situations; coreopsis, *Salvia farinacea*, geranium, verbena and hosta, among others, in a sunny to partly shaded flowerbed.

TURFGRASS

Turfgrass aficionados are having a hard time these days. Many cities are taking steps to ban pesticide use on lawns, and summer water bans leave turf dry and crisp during hot spells. Alternative groundcovers and xeriscapes are being hailed as the way of the future, but there are positives to turfgrasses that make them worth keeping. Lawns efficiently filter pollutants out of run-off water, prevent soil erosion, retain moisture, cool the air and resist drought.

It is possible to have a healthy, attractive organic lawn. Grass is an extremely competitive plant, capable of fighting off invasions by weeds, pests and diseases without the use of chemicals. Watering with compost tea, for example, encourages a healthy lawn and increases pest and disease resistance.

Although lawns require a layer of thatch to improve wear tolerance, reduce compaction and insulate against weather extremes, too thick a thatch layer can prevent water absorption, make the grass susceptible to heat, drought and cold and encourage pest and disease problems. De-thatch lawns in spring only when the thatch layer is more than 3/4" deep.

It is important to note weather variances from season to season. If you do, you will be better prepared for the dips and heights of temperatures. Use this yearbook also for noting the hot and cool spots in your garden. Northern California is notorious for mini-climates from the front to the rear of the garden. Noting these hot or cool spots will help you extend your planting choices.

MAY

22

23

Check your geraniums and petunias for budworms. A simple spray of Bt will put these insects in their place. If you don't wish to spray, you can cover these flowers with a row cover every night and remove in daytime.

24

25

As spring bulbs dry up, remove their tops. Daffodils and narcissus can be left in place. Tulips need to be replanted in the fall. Dig up and toss all of the small ones, but save the good-sized ones in the vegetable compartment of your refrigerator until September. Make sure they are completely dry before refrigerating them.

26

27

28

With their wide variety of leaf shapes, sizes and colors, hostas (*left*) are a popular addition to shaded gardens. *Opposite page, clockwise from top:* penstemon, golden marguerite, basket-of-gold

Here are some tips for maintaining a healthy, organic lawn:

- Aerate your lawn in spring, after active growth begins, to relieve compaction and allow water and air to move freely through the soil.
- Feed the soil, not the plants. Organic fertilizers or compost will encourage a healthy population of soil microbes. These work with roots to provide plants with nutrients and to fight off attacks by pests and diseases. Apply an organic fertilizer every six weeks throughout the year.
- Mow lawns to a height of 2–2¹/₂". If kept this height, the remaining leaf blade will shade the ground, preventing moisture loss, keeping roots cooler, reducing the stress the grass suffers from being mowed and helping the grass out-compete weeds for space and sunlight.
- Grass clippings should be left on the lawn to return their nutrients to the soil and add organic matter. Mowing your lawn once a week or as often as needed during the vigorous growing season will ensure that the clippings decompose quickly.
- Healthy turfgrass will out-compete most weeds. Remove weeds by hand. If you must use chemicals, apply them only to the weeds. Chemical herbicides disrupt the balance of soil microbes and are not necessary to have a healthy lawn.

To keep your perennials and annuals looking their best at this time of year, proper grooming is needed. Allowing seeds to ripen will shorten the life of your annuals and make the perennials unsightly. Old bloom stems of perennials such as penstemon need constant pruning in order to increase subsequent blooms. Shearing marguerites will extend their bloom cycle and keep the plant looking more attractive.

MAY

31

High mountain gardeners should keep checking their local nurseries for blooming perennials that will complement their gardens. By now you can begin to pick your lettuce. Harvest small amounts at a time to extend the bounty.

Though sometimes considered invasive, forget-me-nots (*left*) are easy-to-grow, reliable bloomers and perfect for beginning gardeners. These flowers can be planted all year long in Northern California. Native California lilacs (*top right*) are heat and drought resistant; *Verbascum* and *Euphorbia* among others in a mixed native xeriscape planting at Gamble Gardens (*bottom right*).

Accept that grass will not grow everywhere. Grass requires plenty of sun and regular moisture. Many trees and buildings provide too much shade and don't allow enough water to penetrate the soil for grass to grow successfully. Use mulch or other groundcovers in areas where you have trouble growing grass. When selecting trees to plant in the lawn, choose ones that will provide only light shade and that will enjoy the plentiful water they will be sharing with the grass, or create a grass-free zone extending from the base of the tree to the drip line.

Lawns need regular watering to keep them green and growing. You can best test this by watering well, holding off for a couple of days and then stepping on the grass. If the grass rebounds within an hour, it is not ready for more water. Do this process every day until it no longer rebounds within an hour. Mark these tests in this yearbook and you will have your watering schedule for the rest of the season. Don't fall for the idea that feeding a lawn makes it more thirsty. The opposite is true.

JUNE

The long, warm
days of summer are with us,
and the garden flourishes.

JUNE

The warm weather has made vegetable gardens thrive. It is time to play daily hide-and-seek with your zucchini. If you are noticing fruit not maturing, you may have to do your own pollinating.

If you have some bare spots in your flowerbeds, visit a local nursery for more colorful annuals. Zinnias are great for sunny spots and impatiens work well in shady areas.

Cranesbill geraniums (*left*) are charming late-spring flowers with attractive foliage. The leaves of some species emit a lemon-mint scent. Impatiens and ageratum (*top right*) in a tower planter; daylilies (*bottom right*) planted en masse serve as a screen

School is out and vacations start, but don't ignore the garden. In June, the grass is green, flowerbeds are filling in and perennials, trees and shrubs are blooming. We watch as seeds germinate and leaves unfold. The soil is warm enough for even the most tender plants. All gardeners are watching for dry spells when young and newly planted gardens may need extra water.

THINGS TO DO

If you are planning a vacation, prepare your garden for the time you will be away by mulching, watering and putting your planter boxes and hanging baskets in an area that can be easily watered by a neighbor. This is particularly important if you live in the heat of the Central Valley of Northern California.

Spend some time with your roses. Now is a good time to give them the once over to find any insects you may have not noticed before. The leafcutter bee is out there and disfigures rose leaves by making circular holes on the edges. Not to worry. This beneficial bee will go away shortly. Another feeding with rose food and alfalfa meal or pellets will keep your roses blooming. If you intend to pick your roses for a bouquet, cut them early in the morning. Take them in the house, hold the stems under warm water and make a second cut. Then place them in a vase filled with tepid water. Following this procedure will allow them to last for over two weeks.

Keep cultivating around your trees, shrubs, vegetables and flowers to discourage weeds and allow water to penetrate more deeply around the roots.

Remove dead flowers from plants growing in tubs, window boxes and hanging baskets. Deadheading encourages more flowering and keeps displays looking tidy.

JUNE

Hedges may need special attention at this time
of year. They should be fed and watered
adequately and mulched to protect them
from summer heat.

Think about putting a water feature in your
landscape. If you have raccoons in your
garden, skip putting koi in the pond. They
are considered a very expensive delicacy for
these pesky critters.

Despite the delicate look of its satiny flowers,
godetia (*left*) enjoys the cooler weather of
spring and early summer. Plants often die
back as the summer progresses. Black-
eyed Susans mixed with purple coneflower (*center right*); artemisia
(*bottom right*)

Apply mulch to shrub, perennial and vegetable beds. Doing so will shade the roots and reduce the amount of water the plants will require.

If you suspect insect problems but don't see anything during the day, put out several wet rolled-up newspapers and check them in the early morning. If you discover an insect you are not familiar with, take it to a local nursery in a plastic bag for identification. You may be surprised to find out how many are beneficial.

Pull weeds out of beds when you see them to avoid having to spend an entire day doing it later. A regular weeding regime keeps weeds under control.

Pinch off the faded flowerheads from rhododendrons and azaleas as they finish flowering. Next year's flowers are formed soon after and will be more impressive if the plants are not spending energy producing seeds pods from this year's flowers.

Prune early-flowering shrubs that have finished blooming to encourage the development of young shoots that will bear flowers the following year.

It is a good idea to replace some of the shaggy plants that you put in the ground at the end of spring. Violas, pansies and other annuals are way past their prime. Take a trip to your local nursery and check out what is available. You might just put in a group of lisianthus, which make excellent cut flowers. In all cases replace some of the soil with compost.

Perennials to pinch back:
- Artemisia (*Artemisia* spp.)
- Bee Balm (*Monarda didyma*)
- Black-eyed Susan (*Rudbeckia* spp.)
- Catmint (*Nepeta* hybrids)
- Purple Coneflower (*Echinacea purpurea*)
- Shasta Daisy (*Leucanthemum* hybrids)

JUNE

Plant that second row of sweet corn. If you want pumpkins for October, try the smaller varieties instead of the giant Cinderella type.

If you haven't done so, stake your tomato plants before they grow any bigger. Tomatoes on the ground will rot. If you notice ripe tomatoes on the ground half eaten, chances are roof rats have been dining in your garden, so you might set a rat trap or two.

Coreopsis (*left*) enlivens a summer garden with its bright yellow, continuous blooms. Shear back in late summer for more flowers in fall. *Opposite page, clockwise from top*: flowering maple in a container; ornamental millet with petunias and dahlias; million bells with bidens

It is time to harvest some of your early fruit, such as apricots and cherries. Harvest cherries as soon as you see the first bird harvesting for you. Pick them all at once; they will ripen off the tree. Apricots are of no interest to most birds, but pick them as soon as they show bright orange colors. Check for ants on all of your trees and keep these varmints off with a Tangelfoot™ barrier. Ants are looking at your citrus trees with mites in hand, so keep them out of your citrus and other trees.

Pay particular attention to your citrus trees to keep them clean and fed. They require monthly feeding all year long in Northern California.

One of the biggest problems in the garden at this time of year is fireblight. Anything from pear trees to pyracantha are targets for this virus. If you see dying, darkened branches on any of these members of the rose family, prune them out. Take at least one inch of healthy wood with each cut, and rinse the blades of your pruners with a bleach solution after every cut and again before putting them away. Feeding with fish emulsion on the ground and as a foliar spray will protect the trees and shrubs from further problems.

JUNE

Consider mixing different plants together
in a container. You can create contrasts
of color, texture and habit and give a small
garden an inviting appearance.

As corn and other vegetables mature, plant
a second row for fall harvest. Zucchini will
go until the first frost, but other vegetables
such as lettuce should be replanted on a
continuing program.

The flowers of *Salvia farinacea* 'Victoria' (*left*) are a
beautiful deep violet blue. They look stunning planted
with yellow or orange flowers such as nasturtiums,
California poppies or marigolds. *Opposite page,
clockwise from top left*: graceful petunias lighten a
heavy planter; marigolds, sweet potato vine and
begonias in planters; a deck improved by a lush
container garden; Rangpar lime (*Citrus* x *limonia*)

CONTAINER GARDENING

Most plants can be grown in containers. Annuals, perennials, vegetables, shrubs and even trees can be adapted to container culture.

There are many advantages to gardening in containers:

- They work well in small spaces. Even apartment dwellers with small balconies can enjoy the pleasures of gardening with planters on the balcony.
- They are mobile. Containers can be moved around to take advantage of light or shade and can even be moved into a sheltered location for winter.
- They are easier to reach. Container plantings allow people in wheelchairs or with back problems to garden without having to bend a lot.
- They are useful for extending the season. You can get an early start without the transplant shock that many plants suffer when moved outdoors. You can also protect plants from an early frost in fall.

Put trailing plants near the edge of a container to spill out, and bushy and upright plants in the middle where they will give height and depth to the planting.

JUNE

Keep hydrangeas looking good by eliminating old blooms clear to the base buds of the plant. The subsequent new growth will bloom in nine months.

When planning your vegetable garden, consider planting extra to donate to a local food bank or homeless shelter.

Though considered old-fashioned by some gardeners, petunias (*left*) are versatile and dependable annuals that bloom continuously in any sunny location. New varieties of this flower seem to appear every spring in local nurseries.

In the Sierra mountains, most perennials, shrubs or trees will require more winter protection in containers than they would if grown in the ground. Because the roots are above ground level, they are exposed to the winter wind and cycles of freezing and thawing. Protect container-grown plants by insulating the inside of the pot. Thin sheets of foam insulation can be purchased and fitted around the inside of the pot before the soil is added. Containers can also be moved to sheltered locations. Garden sheds and unheated garages work well to protect plants from the cold and wind of winter.

You can get more than a month's head start on the gardening season by using containers. Tomatoes, pumpkins and watermelons can be started from seed a month before you would traditionally plant them outdoors. Plant them in large containers so they can be moved outside during warm days and brought back in at night as needed until they can be left out overnight. Doing this prevents the stretching that many early-started plants suffer from if kept indoors for too long before being planted into the garden.

Don't do any major pruning on pines until November or December. However, to encourage more compact growth, cut new growth, called candles (*below*), by half.

Some tasks that high mountain gardeners can be doing this month include pruning stems and suckers off old lilacs to keep them vigorous and planting summer-flowering annuals, perennials and vegetables. Include a native *Ceanothus* in your plantings. *Ceanothus*, or California lilac (*top right*), can help prevent soil erosion on slopes, tolerates heat, drought and some frost and winter damage and is generally an undemanding shrub once established.

JULY

July is the
month to relax and enjoy all
of your gardening efforts.

JULY

1

2

Make sure the new growth on all of your vines, including climbing roses, has support.

3

4

Use your own compost or purchased organic fertilizers for container and garden plants.

Happy Birthday USA.
Make a bouquet of red, white and blue flowers.

5

6

7

'Just Joey' (*left*) is a small hybrid tea that grows about 4' high and 36" wide, making it an ideal rose for mixed beds and borders. It bears beautiful, fully double rounded blooms with wavy edges in coppery pink hues. Its flowers are excellent for cutting and garden exhibits.

A riot of phlox, daylilies, yarrow, ageratum and snapdragons (*top right*); a natural-looking water feature (*bottom right*)

Flowerbeds have filled in, green tomatoes ripen on the vine. The season's transplants are established and need less frequent watering. By July, the days are long and warm and the garden appears to grow before your eyes. Some plants can't take the heat and fall dormant while others thrive and fill in the spaces left behind.

THINGS TO DO

Heat and drought can spell disaster for your lawn and garden if you haven't followed good watering practices. Water bans are common in many communities, and frequent, shallow watering earlier in the season creates problems in July when roots unaccustomed to searching deeply for water suffer in its absence.

The hot weather may necessitate more watering and mulching.Water deeply, but no more than once a week during dry spells. Water early in the day to minimize potential disease and reduce water lost through evaporation. Watering late in the day can promote the development of mildew and mold on some plants. If daytime temperatures are hot, water your container plants at least once a day. Apply mulches to the roots of plants to keep them cool and moist.

Pick zucchini when they are small and at their tender and tasty best. Consider donating any extra vegetables to a homeless shelter or food bank, where they will be much appreciated.

To ensure the survival of a new plant in your garden, find out what its optimum growing conditions are, and then plant it where these conditions exist in your yard. For example, don't plant a shrub that needs full sun in a north-facing location.

JULY

8

9

Cultivate around trees, shrubs, vegetable and flower gardens to control weeds and allow better water penetration.

10

11

If vegetable crops are crowded, it is best to thin them out for best production.

Check fishponds and water features during hot weather to make sure evaporation hasn't lowered the water level.

12

13

14

Annual clary sage (*left*) loves sun, and its brilliantly colored bracts attract butterflies and hummingbirds to the flowers. Plant it among other sun-loving annuals and perennials where its whites, pinks and purples will provide bright bursts of color. *Opposite page, clockwise from top left:* porcelain berry; statice; Cape plumbago; bachelor's buttons

Deadhead perennials and annuals as needed to keep them blooming. Remove foliage that was damaged by slugs in the spring. Trim back early-blooming perennials to encourage new foliage growth.

Pick herbs and freeze in envelopes of water for best flavor.

Trim hedges regularly to keep them looking tidy and lush.

If growing peas, pick them and seed new warm-weather plants in their stead. Consider a second crop of corn, and keep planting short rows of leaf lettuce. Nasturtiums planted near your cucumbers will produce fruit that isn't bitter. Don't forget to use nasturtium flowers and leaves in your salads.

In addition to watering, weeding and deadheading, gardeners in the Sierra mountains should be fertilizing trees, shrubs, lawns, roses and any flowering plant about to bloom.

JULY

15

16

Top mulch up if it is getting thin in places in your garden. Mulch protects roots, holds in moisture and helps keep weeds at bay.

17

18

Check the ties on trees and shrubs to make sure the supports aren't cutting into the trunk.

19

20

21

Coreopsis (*left*); use a mixture of annuals and perennials to create garden rooms that add privacy or create paths through the garden (*opposite*).

GARDEN PROBLEMS

Chewed leaves, mildews and nutrient deficiencies tend to become noticeable in July when plants finish their first flush of growth and turn their attention to flowering and fruiting.

Such problems can be minimized if you develop a good problem management program. Though it may seem complicated, problem management is a simple process that relies on correct and timely identification of the problem, then using the least environmentally harmful method to deal with it.

JULY

22

23

Compost piles should get special attention at
this time of year. The warmth of the summer
will speed up decomposition, provided the pile
is turned often and kept moist.

24

25

Trim or shear back early-flowering
perennials when they have
finished blooming.

26

27

28

'Cupcake' (*left*) is a delightful
miniature rose with a classic
hybrid tea shape. It produces an
abundance of blooms and is disease resistant. *Opposite page,
clockwise from top left:* deer-pruned
cedars; a swallowtail on cherry blossoms; a birdbath in a shade garden

Garden problems fall into three basic categories:

- pests, including mollusks such as slugs and snails; insects such as aphids, codling moths, nematodes and whiteflies; and mammals such as mice, rabbits, raccoons and deer

- diseases, caused by bacteria, fungi and viruses

- physiological problems, caused by nutrient deficiencies, too much or too little water and incorrect light levels.

Choose healthy plants that have been developed for their resistance to common problems and that will perform well in the conditions provided by your garden.

Prevention is the most important aspect of problem management. A healthy garden resists problems and develops a natural balance between beneficial and harmful organisms.

JULY

Check climbing vines that have finished blooming. Many of them can be sheared back to force new growth and bloom come the fall.

Cup-and-saucer vine (*below*) produces sweetly scented flowers that are cream colored when they emerge and turn purple as they age. Ladybird beetle (*top right*), a beneficial insect that feasts on aphids; Dahlberg daisies (*bottom right*)

PEST CONTROL

Correct identification of problems is the key to solving them. Just because an insect is on a plant doesn't mean it's doing any harm.

- Cultural controls are the day-to-day gardening techniques you use to keep your garden healthy. Weed, mulch, keep tools clean and grow problem-resistant cultivars to keep your garden healthy.

- Physical controls are the hands-on part of problem solving. Picking insects off leaves, removing diseased foliage and creating barriers to stop rabbits from getting into the vegetable patch are examples of physical controls.

The pesticide industry has responded to consumer demand for effective, environmentally safe pest control products. Biopesticides are made from plant, animal, bacterial or mineral sources. They are effective in small quantities and decompose quickly in the environment. These products may help us reduce our reliance on chemical pesticides.

- Biological controls use natural and introduced populations of predators that prey on pests. Birds, snakes, frogs, spiders, some insects and even bacteria naturally feed on some problem insects. Soil microbes work with plant roots to increase their resistance to disease.

Chemical pest control should always be a last resort. There are many alternatives that pose no danger to gardeners or their families and pets.

For strong, pest-resistant plants, try watering them and spraying their foliage with compost tea.

Compost Tea Recipe: Mix a shovelful of compost in a 5-gallon bucket of water or a bucketful of compost in a 45-gallon barrel of water and let sit for a week. Dilute this mix, preferably with rainwater or filtered water, until it resembles weak tea.

AUGUST

Sit back and enjoy the garden. In the mountains,
summer is at its height while in other areas, this
month is only the halfway point.

AUGUST

Pay special attention to your hanging baskets. Removing old blooms and replacing dead or dying material will pull them through till Thanksgiving.

As some of your annuals fade, visit your local nursery and search for replacement plants. Nursery professionals are always available to answer questions.

Check roses and other plants for powdery mildew. Horticultural oil will cure the problem.

Peruvian lily (*Alstroemeria*) (*left*) grows well under trees or on slopes and blooms for a long time, making it ideal for a mixed border or a cutflower garden. *Opposite page, from top:* geraniums; apples; petunias

With warm days and warm nights still with us, it is time to enjoy the fruits of our spring efforts. Although summer officially started in June, the temperatures will start climbing this month and into the middle of September. August is a great time of year to invite friends and relatives to enjoy a barbecue in the back yard. A swimming pool makes the party even better.

THINGS TO DO

Aside from watering and continued feeding, the garden takes care of itself. Lawns will grow a little faster, but keep the height of your mower to a 2" minimum. Any closer and the grass will be so short that the sun will bake the ground. Set up a croquet or badminton game on your lawn and the kids can invite their friends for a game.

Keep an eye on your fruit trees if they show some stress. It could be that you are overwatering them. Peaches should be harvested by now. Sunflowers should be harvested once you see the birds showing interest.

You have one more chance to plant corn in most areas for an early fall harvest. Another row of lettuce is in order, and you should start thinking about a winter garden. Keep adding material and turning your compost. Make sure to water it occasionally to moisten the beneficial microbes.

Watch for pests that may be planning to hibernate in the debris around your plants or the bark of your trees. Taking care of a few insects now may keep several generations out of your garden next summer.

Your container plants may not be doing well because too much water is sitting in the trays. Put a layer of gravel on the trays, and place the plants on top so that they aren't standing in water.

Now is a good time to go into nurseries to ask for advice. The spring rush is over and vacation time is here, so nursery personnel have more time to spend with clients.

The French marigold (*left*) is just one variety of this popular annual. All marigolds are low-maintenance plants that stand up well to heat, wind and rain.

Continue to water during dry spells. Plants shouldn't need deep watering more than once a week at this time of the year.

Plants such as cranesbill (*top left*), daylilies (*top right*), hens and chicks (*below*) and liatrus (*bottom*) are good plants to divide if you're just starting your perennial collection. They recover and fill in quickly when divided.

Turn the layers of the compost pile and continue to add soil, kitchen scraps and garden debris not diseased or infested with insects.

Avoid pruning rust-prone plants such as mountain ash and crabapple in late summer and fall because many rusts are releasing spores now.

If you are searching catalogs for spring-blooming bulbs, you can make your plans now. The bulbs you saved should be in the vegetable compartment of the refrigerator until you are ready to plant. Tulips and hyacinths should be purchased new each year for best performance in your garden. In the Sierras, these bulbs can be left in the ground and will bloom the next spring. Daffodils and narcissus are a good bet for hillside plantings and need not be dug up each year. They are also gopher proof.

AUGUST

If your shade garden is looking a little stressed, you can still plant impatiens, coleus and other colorful shade-loving plants that will last till the end of October.

Garden chrysanthemums need to be cut back to within 10" of the ground. You can make cuttings and share them with friends. By cutting back and feeding now with organic fertilizer, you will get a compact blooming plant that won't require staking later on.

Zinnias (*below*) are easy to grow, come in a rainbow of colors and make long-lasting cut flowers for floral arrangements. *Opposite page, from top:* sedum and aster are easy to propagate from stem cuttings.

If you are just getting back from vacation, check around your entire yard to make sure everything is moist. No matter how carefully you tell a relative or friend to water, there will always be that special area you know about that they will have forgotten.

You can cut back annuals, such as petunias, that are growing lanky and ugly by half and give them a shot of compost tea or fish emulsion to help them bloom into the fall.

Roses need a check at this time of year. The second crop of aphids will soon appear, so keep track of their habits. If diseases have taken over any of your roses, clean them up now and check your calendar in January for the best times to prune, defoliate and spray lime-sulfur on the plant and the ground to control diseases. A shot of fertilizer now and again in October will give them a boost so you can harvest blooms for the Thanksgiving table.

Keep feeding your citrus trees once a month for best results at harvest time.

High mountain gardeners should divide overgrown perennials and replant them this month so that roots can establish themselves before cold weather arrives. Other gardening tasks this month include harvesting the vegetable garden and setting out fall-flowering plants.

To help prevent summer fires, clear your yard of dry grasses and dead shrubs. Keep piles of wood or other organic debris (e.g., leaves) away from structures.

The easiest cuttings to take from woody plants such as trees, shrubs and vines are called semi-ripe, semi-mature or semi-hardwood cuttings. They are taken from mature new growth that has not become completely woody yet, usually in late summer or early fall.

AUGUST

Keep feeding acid food to all of your azaleas, camellias, rhododendrons and other acid-loving plants until the middle of September.

Check your mollusk population. Snails and slugs are looking for a place to winter and lay their eggs. If you keep putting out Sluggo™, you will catch them before they can multiply.

Lion's tail (*left*) is a bold-looking drought-tolerant perennial that combines well with Mexican sage. It blooms in August. *Opposite page, clockwise from top:* moonflower; nasturtiums with creeping Jenny; zinnias

Below is a list of plants you can collect seeds or take cuttings from easily. Avoid F1 hybrids, which will not come true from seed.

- Daylilies (*Hemerocallis* spp.)
- Dwarf Dahlia (*Dahlia* spp.)
- Hollyhock (*Alcea* spp.)
- Impatiens (*Impatiens* spp.)
- Mallow (*Lavatera* spp.)
- Morning Glory (*Ipomoea* spp.)
- Nasturtium (*Tropaeolum majus*)
- Poppy (*Papaver rhoeas*)
- Zinnia (*Zinnia elegans*)

PLANT PROPAGATION

August is a good time to propagate plants. Taking cuttings and gathering seed are great ways to increase your plant collection and to share some of your favorite plants with friends and family.

Now is a good time to divide some perennials and to note which of your plants will need dividing next spring. Look for these signs that perennials need dividing:

- The center of the plant has died out.

- The plant is no longer flowering as profusely as it did in previous years.

- The plant is encroaching on the growing space of other plants.

Perennials, trees, shrubs and tender perennials that are treated like annuals can all be started from cuttings. This method is an excellent way to propagate varieties and cultivars that you really like but that are slow or difficult to start from seed or that don't produce viable seed.

Seeds of different species have different shelf lives. Check seed catalogs or seed packages for information on how long different seeds will last.

Nasturtiums (*below*) are versatile annuals. Their edible flowers and foliage are attractive additions to baskets and containers as well as to salads. Even the seedpods can be pickled and used as a substitute for capers. *Opposite page, clockwise from top left:* drying poppy seedheads; golden clematis flowers and seedheads

There is some debate over what size cuttings should be. Some people claim that smaller cuttings are more likely to root and will root more quickly. Others claim that larger cuttings develop more roots and become established more quickly once planted. Try different sizes and see what works best for you.

Always make cuttings just below a leaf node (the point where the leaf attaches to the stem).

Many gardeners enjoy the hobby of collecting and planting seed. You need to know a few basic things before you begin:

- Know your plant. Correctly identify the plant and learn about its life cycle. You will need to know when it flowers, when the seeds are likely to ripen and how the plant disperses its seeds in order to collect them.

- Find out if there are special requirements for starting the seeds. For example, do they need a hot or cold period to germinate?

When collecting seed, consider the following:

- Collect seeds once they are ripe but before they are shed from the parent plant.

- Remove capsules, heads or pods as they begin to dry and remove the seeds later, once they are completely dry.

- Place a paper bag over a seedhead as it matures and loosely tie it in place to collect seeds as they are shed.

- Dry seeds after they've been collected. Place them on a paper-lined tray and leave them in a warm, dry location for one to three weeks.

- Separate seeds from the other plant parts and clean them before storing.

- Store seeds in air-tight containers in a cool, frost-free location.

Depending on the size of your perennials, you can divide them using a shovel or pitchfork (for large plants), a sharp knife (for small plants) or your hands (for easily divided plants).

Don't collect seeds or plants from wild areas because wild harvesting is severely depleting many plant populations. Many species and populations of wild plants are protected, and it is illegal to collect their seeds.

SEPTEMBER

Warm weather continues in all areas but the Sierras, where there might be a touch of frost in the latter part of this month.

SEPTEMBER

1

2

Resist the temptation to cut back ornamental grasses. Save that task till February.

3

4

Spray zinnias, asters and other blooming plants prone to mildew with horticultural oil.

5

6

7

Strawflower (*left*), ornamental grasses (*top right*) and amaranthus (*center right*) can be harvested now for dried flower arrangements. Crape myrtle (*bottom right*)

Leaves may begin to change color, ripening seedheads nod in the breeze and brightly colored berries and fruit adorn many trees and shrubs. This is usually quite a dry month for coastal gardens, while gardeners in the Central Valley will enjoy the revival of many plants with the cooler nights.

THINGS TO DO

Having enjoyed another summer garden, some of the fall clean up begins.

Take advantage of end-of-season sales. Many garden centers are getting rid of trees, shrubs and perennials at reduced prices. There is still plenty of time for the roots to become established before the ground freezes. Do not buy plants that are excessively pot-bound and avoid planting in hot weather, which will stress new transplants.

Start planting seeds for the winter garden. In flats, sow sweet peas, cabbage, cauliflower, Brussels sprouts, Chinese cabbage and broccoli to plant at the end of this month.

SEPTEMBER

8

9

Check your hummingbird feeders. Make sure they are clean, and rinse in mild bleach solution to kill any disease.

10

11

Planting trees and shrubs in the fall gives them a better start come spring.

12

13

14

Big leaf hydrangea (*left*) is a popular shrub that needs protection from hot afternoon sun. It thrives in all shady locations in Northern California. The spent blooms can be dried for flower arrangements. *Opposite page, clockwise from top left:* the fall colors and features of Chinese pistache, Japanese maple, ginkgo and burning bush

If you've let your weeds get out of hand over summer, pull them up before they set seed to avoid having even more weeds popping up in the garden next summer. Avoid tossing weeds that have gone to seed into your compost heap. If your compost isn't hot enough, the seeds will germinate when you add the compost to your garden.

The spent flowers of perennials, dead or dying annuals, fruit from trees and other material need to be cleaned up now to prevent any disease or insects from wintering over. Keep all plants, but especially young fruit trees, well watered.

The changing colors are a sure sign that fall is here. Bright reds, golds, bronzes and coppers seem to give warmth to a cool day. The display doesn't have to be reserved for a walk in the park. Include trees and shrubs with good fall color such as those listed here to your garden:

- Burning Bush (*Euonymus alatus*)
- Cotoneaster (*Cotoneaster* spp.)
- Maples (*Acer* spp.)
- Virginia Creeper (*Parthenocissus quinquefolia*)
- Witch-hazel (*Hamamelis* spp.)

SEPTEMBER

15

16

In the Sierra mountains, the first frost will affect tomato, pepper and other frost-sensitive vegetables. Harvest as much fruit as you can and allow it to ripen in the house.

17

18

Maintain your watering. Cool weather will follow the heat spike this month, so don't let the landscape dry out.

19

20

The cheery golden marguerite daisy plant (*below*) forms a tidy mound that works wonderfully in both formal and informal garden settings. *Opposite page, clockwise from top left:* Asiatic lily 'Electra'; fancy tulip; 'Monte Carlo' tulips; black-eyed Susan

21

Bulbs are available in all nurseries. Plant at the end of this month into October. Add bulb food to all bulbs, and condition soil with plenty of compost or planting mix. Don't refrigerate newly purchased bulbs because they have already been chilled. Plant bulbs in containers to grow for later on if you have no space in the garden. When the flowers bloom, you can plant the containers in the ground for an instant display.

Fall and winter flowers such as violas, pansies, Iceland poppies, calendula and candytuft make excellent covers for bulb beds. Your local nurseries will have starts of all of these.

Mountain gardeners can harvest vegetables and plant colorful fall ornamentals such as chrysanthemums, flowering cabbage and kale and spring-blooming bulbs such as snowdrops, daffodils and tulips. Move tender container plants into a sheltered location to protect from frost. Many annuals are undamaged by early frosts and continue to bloom until the first hard freeze. Divide and plant perennials now so they can put down roots before the soil freezes.

SEPTEMBER

22

23

It is time to do a light pruning of all of your fruit trees in case branches have broken from too much fruit. Budded camellias can be pruned at this time of year.

24

If you are into wildflowers, this is the time to scatter the seed. California poppies and California lupines are favorites. Make sure wildflower mixes contain these two flowers. If there is rain and then a dry spell, make sure you water if seeds have sprouted.

25

26

27

28

Echinacea purpurea (left), commonly called purple coneflower and used as a popular herbal cold remedy, is a long-blooming, drought-resistant perennial. Its distinctively cone-shaped flowers look good in fresh and dried floral arrangements.

CREATING WILDLIFE HABITAT

The rapid and relentless rate of urban sprawl has led to the loss of wildlife habitat. Our gardens can easily provide some of the space, shelter, food and water that wildlife needs. Here are a few tips for creating a wildlife-friendly garden:

- Make sure at least some of the plants in your garden are locally native. Birds and small animals are used to eating native plants, so they'll visit a garden that has them. When selecting non-native plants for your yard, choose those that wildlife might also find appealing, such as shrubs that bear fruit.

- Provide a source of water. A pond with a shallow side or a birdbath will offer water for drinking and bathing. Frogs and toads eat a wide variety of insect pests and will happily take up residence in or near a ground-level water feature.

This page: Birdbaths, birdfeeders, tall flowering perennials such as lupins (*top*), Joe Pye weed (*left*), and annuals attract wildlife to your yard.

SEPTEMBER

*If you are thinking of putting in a new lawn
or refurbishing your present lawn,
now is an excellent time to do it.*

The zinnia (*below*) is named after Johann Gottfried Zinn (1727–59), a German botany professor who started growing these South American flowers from seed in Europe. *Opposite page, clockwise from top left:* birdfeeder; bee balm with butterfly; sunflower; flycatcher on a cherry tree

- A variety of birdfeeders and seed will encourage different species of birds to visit your garden. Some birds will visit an elevated feeder, but others prefer a feeder set at or near ground level. Fill your feeders regularly—birds always appreciate a reliable food source, especially when their natural food sources are low or scarce.

- Shelter is the final aspect to keeping your resident wildlife happy. Patches of dense shrubs, tall grasses and mature trees provide shelter. As well, you can leave a small pile of twiggy brush in an out-of-the-way place. Nature stores and many garden centers sell toad houses and birdhouses.

It is a good idea to collect fallen fruit because it may attract unwanted wildlife, such as rats, skunks, raccoons and coyotes, to your garden.

Butterflies, hummingbirds and a wide variety of predatory insects will be attracted if you include lots of pollen-producing plants in your garden. Plants such as comfrey, bee balm, salvia, Joe Pye weed, black-eyed Susan, catmint, purple coneflower, coreopsis, hollyhock and yarrow will attract pollen lovers.

OCTOBER

October sees the final burst of blooming and
harvesting in the mountains while the rest of
Northern California will bask in Indian Summer.

OCTOBER

1

2

Planting bulbs this month will guarantee spring
blooms. Use lots of compost and bulb food
for best results.

3

4

Much of the summer garden is ready
for the compost pile, but for most areas,
a fall planting is in order.

5

6

In the Sierra mountains the frost dominates,
so yard clean-up is order. Other areas of
Northern California need a harvest clean-
up and a fall planting of vegetables.

7

Make sure the harvest is finished on ripe fruit
such as apples (*left*) and pears. *Opposite
page, from top:* pomegranate;
fresh-picked carrots

Most gardens are still vigorous in early October, but by Halloween, many are showing signs of the onslaught of winter. In the Sierras, you can plant spinach seeds and let the winter snow cover them. By April you will have a fine crop of greens. Other Northern California gardeners can be harvesting and planting more lettuce, root crops, cabbage, broccoli and Brussels sprouts. All gardeners can be shopping for spring-blooming bulbs and native plants now when the selection is good.

THINGS TO DO

Raking leaves will now become a weekend job until the first rains or snow in November. Don't let them collect because they will set up fungal problems come spring. Before putting them into your compost pile, grind them up by running a lawnmower over them several times. It is best to do this on your driveway or another area with a solid base.

Mowing your lawn to no less than 1¹/₂" and feeding it with a low nitrogen or organic fertilizer will let it jump into spring as a dark green carpet. Coastal gardeners can seed a new lawn, but sow seeds before heavy rains wash seeds away.

Groundcovers and other landscape areas can be weed free come spring by an application this month of a seed inhibitor. Annual blue grass (*Poa annua*) can be one of the most common grasses in all landscape areas, and because it seeds so heavily, it should not be ignored. Pre-emergent products are safe and available for application this month.

In colder areas, unless your plants have some sort of disease, you can leave faded perennial growth in place and clean it up in spring. The stems will collect leaves and snow, protecting the roots and crown of the plant over the winter.

OCTOBER

8

9

Fall is the time to plant trees, shrubs
and lawns. If you are planning major
landscaping, this is the time of year to take
advantage of the winter rains.

10

11

Wildflowers sown at this time will have a
good chance of sprouting come spring. Make
sure they are watered if the rains fail.

Check local farmers' markets for a good
selection of seasonal vegetables and flowers.

12

13

14

Pomegranate (*left*) not only produces wonderful
fuchsia-like orange flowers all spring and summer, it also bears ornamental and edible fruit
(*see previous page*). *Opposite page, clockwise
from top:* flannel bush, Monterey cypress,
monkey flower

Tuberous begonias should be lifted and stored only after the top growth has separated itself from the tuber. Dahlias, gladiolas and other tubers and bulbs should be dug out at this time. Lift them out and wash the dirt off them thoroughly. Rinse them in a solution of bleach (3 tablespoons per gallon), and allow to dry before storing in brown paper bags.

Cure winter squash, such as acorn squash, pumpkins and spaghetti squash, in a cool, frost-free location before storing for winter.

If you haven't kept your mums pinched back, you will need to stake them. Divide other perennials that are finished blooming and share with neighbors or add them to your garden.

Tomatoes can produce vine-ripe flavor even in cooler temperatures. To extend the harvest time, pick them just as they turn color and ripen them on a sunny windowsill (not the refrigerator). Excess moisture can spread tomato blight; a fungus that quickly kills tomatoes. In areas of high rainfall, shelter plants to keep them dry. Mulching may also help keep water off plants and fruit.

If some of your vine crops are showing signs of mildew, make a tea from your compost and spray the foliage to return stressed plants to health. Use one pound of compost to one gallon of water, let stand in the sun for two days and use the resulting liquid as a fungicide.

Native plant societies hold their sales this month. October is also the best month for setting out native trees, shrubs and perennials. Some to try are

- California Lilac (*Ceanothus*)
- Coast Redwood (*Seqouia sempervirens*)
- Flannel Bush (*Fremontodendron*)
- Monkey Flower (*Mimulus*)
- Pacific Coast Iris (*Iris douglasiana*)
- Western Redbud (*Ceris occidentalis*)
- Yarrow (*Achillea millefolium*)

15

16

Continue garden clean-up. Make sure dead blooms around camellias are removed to prevent blossom blight. The last feeding for these plants should take place now.

17

18

Now is the time of year to make a shopping expedition to your local nursery for new and unusual plants that might be added to your landscape. Many arboretums have plant sales, and now is a good time to visit them.

19

20

21

Honeysuckle vine (*left*) flowers from summer to fall frost. Prune in spring to cut back dead growth as new leaves emerge. *Opposite page, from top:* eucalyptus provides flowers and interesting bark in the landscape; bins for different stages of composting; composting materials

Clean all spent garden materials, such as corn stalks, chop them up and put them in the compost pile. Store all winter squash in a cool, dry area for winter. If you haven't done so, plant spinach, cauliflower, cabbage and other winter crops at this time. Beets, carrots and other root crops can be seeded now for an early spring harvest.

Some perennials can be divided now. Mid- to late summer bloomers will probably flower next summer if divided now. Don't divide spring and early summer bloomers because the shock of division may prevent them from flowering next year.

Mountain gardeners should be cleaning up and storing hoses and flushing irrigation systems, harvesting the last of the vegetables, pulling up dying annuals and applying a thick layer of mulch to protect vulnerable perennials or taking them indoors for overwintering.

COMPOSTING

One of the best additives for any type of soil is compost. Compost can be purchased at most garden centers, and many communities now have composting programs. You can easily make compost in your own garden. Though garden refuse and vegetable scraps from your kitchen left in a pile will eventually decompose, it is possible to produce compost more quickly. Here are a few suggestions for making compost:

- Compost decomposes most quickly when there is a balance between dry and fresh materials. There should be more dry matter (chopped straw or shredded leaves) than green matter (vegetable scraps and grass clippings).

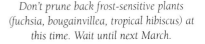

22

23

Don't prune back frost-sensitive plants (fuchsia, bougainvillea, tropical hibiscus) at this time. Wait until next March.

24

25

If seasonal rains haven't taken over the watering, continue to replenish the water in your landscape. This is especially important under the eaves of the house and in areas where rains can't reach.

26

27

28

Yarrow's showy, flat-topped flowerheads (*left*) provide months of continuous color in summer, and the seedheads persist into winter. They can be added to dry flower arrangements.

- The addition of red worms to your pile can increase the rate of decomposition.
- Layer the dry and the green matter, and mix in some garden soil or previously finished compost. This step introduces decomposer organisms to the pile.
- Compost won't decompose properly if it is too wet or too dry. Keep the pile covered during heavy rain, and sprinkle it with water if it is too dry. The correct level of moisture can best be described as that of a wrung-out sponge.
- To aerate the compost pile, use a garden fork to poke holes in it or turn it regularly. Use a thermometer with a long probe attached, similar to a large meat thermometer, to check the temperature in your pile. When it reaches 158° F, give the pile a turn.

Images of fall (*clockwise*): ginger lily; passiflora; juicy clusters of vine-ripened grapes; tasty corn on the cob fresh from the garden. Many gardeners find fruiting plants to be decorative as well as useful.

OCTOBER

29

30

31

Besides keeping the lawn mowed, make sure to cultivate around the flower beds and trees and shrubs to allow the winter rains to penetrate deeper into the soil. Adding chicken manure to fruit trees and small fruits will encourage more fruit next year.

Sunflowers (*below*) are synonymous with fall for many gardeners. Their bold yellow, seed-filled flowerheads celebrate the harvest season and provide treats for the birds. *Opposite page, clockwise from top:* heavenly bamboo; viburnum; yarrow

Before adding any amendments to your soil, you should get a soil test done. Simple kits to test for pH and major nutrients are available at garden centers. More thorough tests are done at government or private labs. These tests will tell you what the pH is, the comparative levels of sand, silt, clay and organic matter and the quantities of all required nutrients. They will also tell you what amendments to add and in what quantities to improve your soil.

- Finished compost is dark in color and light in texture. When you no longer recognize what went into the compost, it is ready for use.
- Compost can be mixed into garden soil or spread on the surface as a mulch.
- If you haven't got the time or the inclination to fuss over your compost, you can just leave it in a pile, and it will eventually decompose with no added assistance from you.
- In areas with mild winters, open compost piles may attract rodents. To prevent this from happening, store compost in a plastic bin.

There are other good amendments for soil, depending on what is required:
- Alfalfa, your compost and even horse manure can be added to your soil in the fall to loosen the soil structure and allow better water penetration when winter rains start.
- If you have taken a pH test and find your soil either acidic or alkaline, you can correct the pH by adding soil sulfur to correct alkalinity, and oyster-shell lime to correct acidic soil. The latter also prevents blossom end rot on tomatoes.

Many native California plants such as yarrow (*Achillea millefolium*) (*above*) are able to withstand rainless summers quite well. Check your local native plant society for the newest cultivars.

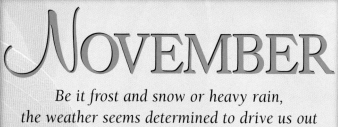

NOVEMBER

Be it frost and snow or heavy rain,
the weather seems determined to drive us out
of the garden this month.

NOVEMBER

1

2

Store unused seed for the garden in air-tight plastic containers and place in the refrigerator or a cool garage for next season.

3

4

Make sure outdoor plants (e.g., bonsai) in containers are not in saucers full of water during the winter. Fill trays with rocks and place plants on top to keep roots from drowning.

Never use just plain plastic to protect plants from frost because it provides no insulation.

5

6

7

Prickly poppy (*left*) self-seeds, so it may pop up from year to year in the same area if left to its own devices. *Opposite page, clockwise from top left:* bonsai; camellia; loquat

There are lots of flowers that can be planted now to perk up your yard during the winter. It is still not too late to plant some colorful flowers available now in nurseries. Try Iceland poppies, pansy, viola, calendula and primrose for exceptional color during the winter. You can get away with another planting of lettuce in the vegetable garden. Spinach and Swiss chard are other green vegetables that can be harvested during the winter months.

Heavy rain can create serious problems in your garden. Some strategies to improve drainage include digging trenches to divert run-off, stabilizing garden beds by using rocks, or planting hardy shrubs or flowers on bald spots to absorb excess water.

THINGS TO DO

The garden tasks this time are limited by how many rainy days there are. Snow bunnies are itching for snow in the Sierras so they won't be much help in the garden. But the leaves must still be raked, lawns mowed and weeds pulled, and these duties can act as a carrot for those who will furnish the transportation.

All root crops can be left in the garden and harvested as needed. Protect frost-sensitive plants such as hibiscus, bougainvillea and citrus by applying an anti-desiccant on the foliage. If real frost hits, cover these plants with burlap, blankets or old drapes but not plain plastic.

NOVEMBER

8

9

Clean up any broken branches on your fruit
trees now before winter sets in.

10

11

Clean up the spent blooms on your pansies
and violas to prevent bacteria from infecting
future blooms.

12

13

14

The hybrid tea 'Paradise' (*left*) is an ideal cut flower;
its graceful, long, pointed buds are borne on tall,
sturdy stems. Considered one of the best lavender-
toned roses available, it looks best in warm climates,
but keep it out of intense sun. The richly colored
rosettes of ornamental kale (*top right*) are reminis-
cent of roses such as 'Hénri Martin' (*far right*).

Turn off your drip irrigation systems and drain them to prevent any winter damage. Next spring make sure you check for insects in the system that may have used these comfortable environs as a winter nesting place.

Make sure your hummingbird feeders are clean and restocked. This may be their only source of food during the winter months. Clean and sterilize all birdfeeders, including hummingbird feeders, every two weeks to prevent the spread of diseases.

Make sure all of your succulent plants, which are normally drought proof, have proper drainage during the rainy seasons. If they tend to collect water around the root system during a rainstorm, cultivate the soil to aerate the root system.

Biennial seeds can be broadcasted at this time with the promise of flowers come next fall. Hollyhocks and perennial foxgloves are good prospects.

Most roses will give their last spurt of flowers this month. If you have fed them properly, you should be able to pick a bouquet for the Thanksgiving table. A final addition of alfalfa meal or pellets will soak into the ground to prepare them for a burst of growth next spring.

Strawberry beds should be groomed at this time of year to clean up any dead or diseased foliage. A light mulching of cedar bark (*above*) will deter slug damage during the winter months.

NOVEMBER

15

16

Put out snail and slug bait around
your lettuce plants to prevent
unwanted guests in the foliage.

17

18

Continue to shop for plants if you wish
to change parts of your landscape.
Trees planted now will grow more
successfully next year.

19

20

21

Red-hot poker (*left*) blooms mid-summer to fall, needing
only a modest amount of water during the summer.
Opposite page, clockwise from top left: yucca and black-
eyed Susan; prickly pear cactus; agave; *Euphorbia lambii*

PROBLEM AREAS

If an area of your garden always seems dry, consider a xeriscape planting in that area. Many plants, especially native ones, are drought resistant and thrive even in areas that are never watered. Black-eyed Susan, cosmos, hollyhock, jack pine, lilac, potentilla, prickly pear cactus, yarrow and yucca are just a few of the many possibilities.

Now that you've had the chance to observe your garden for a growing season, consider the microclimates and think about how you can put them to good use. Are any areas always quick to dry? Do some areas stay wet longer than others? What area is the most sheltered? Which is the least sheltered? Design your plantings around the many microclimates of your garden.

NOVEMBER

23

Daylilies and other perennials may need a final clean up before winter really sets in. Try your hand at saving some of the seed and creating new and interestingly colored flowers.

It is time to turn your attention to your houseplants. Make sure they are not standing in water in their trays. A final washing down of all the foliage in the bathtub will help them survive the heat of a dry winter house.

26

Flowers such as marsh marigold (*left*), daylily and iris (*opposite page, top right*), ligularia (*center right*) and meadowsweet (*bottom right*) work well in damp areas of the garden because they prefer moist growing conditions.

BOG GARDENING

Turn a damp area into your own little bog garden. Dig out an area 14–20" below ground level, line with a piece of punctured pond liner and fill with soil. The area will stay wet but still allow some water to drain away, providing a perfect location to plant moisture-loving perennials. A few to consider are:

- Astilbe (*Astilbe* x *arendsii*)
- Cardinal Flower (*Lobelia* x *speciosa*)
- Daylily (*Hemerocallis* hybrids)
- Doronicum (*Doronicum orientale*)
- Goat's Beard (*Aruncus dioicus*)
- Hosta (*Hosta* hybrids)
- Iris (*Iris ensata* and *I. siberica*)
- Lady's Mantle (*Alchemilla mollis*)
- Ligularia (*Ligularia dentata* and *L. wilsoniana*)
- Marsh Marigold (*Caltha palustris*)
- Meadowsweet (*Filipendula rubra* and *F. ulmaria*)
- Primrose (*Primula japonica*)
- Rodgersia (*Rodgersia aesculifolia*)

Another planting idea for your enjoyment is to create an herb garden. Many winter-hardy herbs such as rosemary and sage can add a picked-fresh flavor to any meal.

If you are interested in plants that feature fall color, now's the time to visit your local nurseries to see what's in stock.

NOVEMBER

30

*Consider consulting a certified arborist
if you have trees with heavy limbs growing
over your home or garden.*

The butterfly bush (*left*) makes a beautiful addition
to a shrub or mixed border. Its graceful, arching
branches make it an excellent specimen plant.
Opposite page, clockwise from top left: Oregon
grape holly, rock rose, winter jasmine, pieris, loquat

Checking your microclimates may well give you a larger selection of tropical and semi-tropical plants that you can grow in your garden. I have seen banana palms thrive in Pennsylvania, where the winters get quite cold. Mulching is the key to this success. Other plants such as Canna lilies, clump bamboo, citrus, loquats, ginger and palms can thrive in some areas of your garden and give you that tropical feeling.

Fruit trees will benefit from a generous addition of chicken manure worked into the ground at this time. Winter rains will allow this material to penetrate deeply into the ground. Continue to feed citrus trees throughout the winter. If you have yellow leaves, add liquid iron and zinc to the soil.

Feed your lawn with an organic fertilizer every six weeks through the winter. This will keep it healthy without forcing top growth that will require mowing.

DECEMBER

The joy of the holidays makes summer seem
far away. Winter color is coming into full bloom,
reducing the gray of rain clouds.

DECEMBER

1

2

The leaves from Liquidambar and other colorful fall leaves make wonderful dry floral arrangements for the season.

3

4

If winter rains have slowed down, don't forget to add your own water. This is especially true for sprouting wildflower seeds.

5

6

7

Holly (*left*) puts on a dependable show of colorful fruit in late fall—just in time for Christmas. It makes a great hedge, shrub border or specimen plant. *Opposite page, from top:* poinsettia; holly foliage; snow on spruce

As the light of the sun shifts lower in the sky and houses become closed and warmer, our thoughts turn from outdoors to indoors, to Christmas decorations, meal planning for the holidays and other joys of the season. Snow in the mountains urges us to forget our gardens. Not so with many gardeners, who are already planning the January joys of the garden that will beckon us outside. Only stormy weather prevents us from answering the call. We can expect some frost to put the final death notice to tomato and pepper plants we have yet to pull. We must protect our citrus if the weather becomes frosty. Now is also a good time to apply dormant spray to trees and shrubs to protect them from over-wintering diseases and insects.

THINGS TO DO

If you haven't already done so, store your tools for the winter. Use a light machine oil on shovel heads and hoes to prevent rust. The lawnmower won't be used for a while, so now is a good time to have it serviced. Remove the gas before storing it away.

Most of the stubborn leaves now cover the ground. Rake them up at the first break in the weather.

If you saved some of your basil for over-wintering, keep it in the sunniest location possible. Other herbs are hardy in Northern California and need very little attention.

If you planted a fall vegetable garden, you can reward yourself with fresh garden vegetables such as cabbage, broccoli, Brussels sprouts, lettuce, root crops and perhaps a ripe persimmon still hanging from the tree.

DECEMBER

8

9

Remove any mulch from around the trunks
of trees. This will prevent problems such
as damage from excessive moisture.

10

11

Now is a good time to shop for houseplants
that will help green up the home during
the dull months of winter. Make sure to ask
about the lighting needs of each plant before
you purchase any of them.

12

13

Phalaenopsis (left) and (*opposite page, clockwise
from top*) *Cattelya*, *Meltonia* and *Cymbidium* orchids
are among the favorites for orchid lovers in Northern
California. Most require only weekly watering and
fertilizing. *Cymbidiums* can be left outside in a protected spot over the winter, but other orchids may
require special attention in cold weather.

14

Clean out the gutters to keep overflow from making divots in the landscape, and direct the water from downspouts so that it doesn't damage any areas of the yard.

Pine trees and other conifers are at their most dormant now, so this is the best time to prune them. Windowing (thinning out entire branches) will prevent them from damaging the landscape should winter winds become violent and cause them to break or fall.

Your favorite fruit trees need to be protected from roof rats. They usually gnaw at the base of the tree and can kill the cambium layer. Place rat traps out early to detect their presence. Use peanut butter on the underside of the trigger as bait.

Rabbits and deer can be a problem, so protect the bark of young trees with corrugated drain material or surround the trunks with leaf-filled wire barriers.

High mountain gardeners who haven't already done so should protect any woody, tender shrubs and perennials that go dormant by covering their roots with a thick layer of mulch. You can also prune a few branches from pines, junipers and other red-berried plants to use as holiday greens for your home.

Houseplants are more than just attractive—they clean the air in our homes. Many dangerous and common toxins, such as benzene, formaldehyde and trichloroethylene, are absorbed and eliminated by houseplants.

DECEMBER

15

16

Check under the eaves to make sure any plants growing there are getting enough water through the fall and winter.

17

18

If you have a bright light situation in the house, Ficus benjamina *can bring a tower of green into the home.*

19

20

21

When selecting a poinsettia (*left*), make sure that the little buds at the top of the plant are tight and not open, so they will show their color for a longer period of time. Spider plant (*top right*)

HOUSEPLANT CARE

As the heat in the house goes on, the moisture of the air declines. An occasional trip to the shower to rinse house dust off their foliage will benefit all your houseplants. Do not use leaf shine to make the plants look shiny—they will resent it. If a lot of dust has coated the leaves, wipe off the upper surface with skim milk. Feed with every watering by cutting the recommended amount of fertilizer in half. Always allow plants to drain before placing them back into a tray. Never let them stand in a tray full of water.

Just as you did for the garden outdoors, match your indoor plants to the conditions your home provides.

Plants that like humid conditions, such as African violets, ferns and philodendrons may do best in your bathroom, where water from showering and the toilet bowl maintain higher moisture levels than in other rooms. Plants that tolerate or prefer dry air, such as cacti, ficus, palms and poinsettias, grow well with no added humidity.

If you're tired of poisettias, try an azalea, cyclamen or Jerusalem cherry for a dash of holiday color indoors. Azaleas can be planted outdoors later in spring.

Look for creative ways to display your plants and add beauty to your home. Indoor fountains and moisture-loving plants, such as a peace lily in a vase of water (*right*), are interesting and attractive. They add a decorative touch to a houseplant display.

DECEMBER

22

23

Many non-traditional plants will bring color
and joy as gifts to some of your favorite
people. Cyclamen, amaryllis, azaleas,
paperwhites and orchids lead the list
for other-than-poinsettia gifts.

24

25

26

27

28

English wallflower (*left*) blooms in winter.
Opposite page, from top: Exbury Hybrid azalea;
gerbera daisies

There are three aspects of interior light to consider: intensity, duration and quality. Intensity is the difference between a south-facing window with full sun and a north-facing room with no direct sunlight. Duration is how long the light lasts in a specific location. An east-facing window will have a shorter duration of light than a south-facing window. Quality refers to the spectrum of the light. Natural light provides a broader spectrum than artificial light. Chances are, if you can't take a black and white picture of the area, no plant will do well.

Watering is a key element to houseplant care. Over-watering can be as much of a problem as under-watering. As you did with your garden plants, water thoroughly and infrequently. Let the soil dry out a bit before watering plants. Some plants are the exception to this rule. Find out what the water requirements of your houseplants are so you will have an idea of how frequently or infrequently you will need to water.

Houseplants generally only need fertilizer when they are actively growing. Always use a weak fertilizer to avoid burning the roots. Never feed plants when they are very dry. Moisten the soil by watering and then feed a couple of days later.

When repotting, go up by only one size at a time. In general, the new pot should be no more than 2–4" larger in diameter than the previous pot. If you find your soil drying out too frequently, then you may wish to use a larger pot that will stay moist for longer.

Here are a few easy-to-grow, toxin-absorbing houseplants:

- Bamboo Palm (*Camaedorea erumpens*)
- Chinese Evergreen (*Aglaonema modestum*)
- Dragon Tree (*Dracaena marginata*)
- English Ivy (*Hedera helix*)
- Gerbera Daisy (*Gerbera jamesonii*)
- Peace Lily (*Spathiphyllum* 'Mauna Loa')
- Pot Mum (*C.* x *morifolium*)
- Snake Plant (*Sansevieria trifasciata*)
- Spider Plant (*Chlorophytum cosmosum*)
- Weeping Fig (*Ficus benjamina*)

DECEMBER

Ants around your houseplants may be an indication that insects have found their way to your favorites. Check with your local nursery for advice.

Happy New Year!

Helleborus niger, or Christmas rose (*below*) is the perfect plant for shady areas where bold foliage is needed. Its subtle colors and delicate appearance brighten sheltered borders or rock and woodland gardens. Rubber plant (*top right*)

Keep in mind that many common house-plants are tropical and dislike hot, dry conditions. Most houseplants will thrive in cooler, moister conditions than you will provide in your home. Always turn thermostats down at night and provide moist conditions by sitting pots on pebble trays. Water in the pebble tray can evaporate but won't soak excessively into the soil of the pot because the pebbles hold it above the water. Coastal garden-ers may not have problems providing sufficient humidity for houseplants, but they do need to provide more light, so keep plants near windows.

Plants can be grouped together in large containers to more easily meet the needs of the plants. Cacti can be planted together in a gritty soil mix and placed in a dry, bright location. Moisture- and humidity-loving plants can be planted in a large terrarium where moisture lev-els remain higher.

Football is king at this time of year, so inside as well as outside gardening is going to take a backseat. If you are having a group over for New Year's Day, or planning a party of any sort, make sure the entry to your home is loaded with potted plants, which are available at most nurseries right after the 25th. You may have already predicted this by having pots of winter color available in other parts of your garden. If your eyes get blurry from watching too much TV, go outside and turn the compost pile. The other alternative is to sharpen your pruning tools so they are finely honed before the duties of January come calling.

Fernleaf acacia (*above*) is a perfect shade tree for dry, hot spots in the landscape. It also works well as a feature tree. Acacia's fragrant flowers are attractive in floral arrangements, especially combined with spring-flowering bulbs.

RESOURCES

All resources cited were accurate at the time of publication. Please note that addresses, phone numbers and web sites/e-mail may change over time.

BOOKS

Acorn, John and Ian Sheldon. 2002. *Bugs of Northern California.* Lone Pine Publishing, Edmonton, AB.

Brenzel, Kathleen Norris, ed. 2001. *Western Garden Book.* Sunset Publishing, Menlo Park, CA.

Creasy, Rosalind. 1982. *The Complete Book of Edible Landscaping.* University of California Press, Berkeley, CA.

Courtier, Jane and Graham Clarke. 1997. *Indoor Plants: The Essential Guide to Choosing and Caring for Houseplants.* Reader's Digest, Westmount, PQ.

Ellis, B.W. and F.M. Bradley, eds. 1996. *The Organic Gardener's Handbook of Natural Insect and Disease Control.* Rodale Press, Emmaus, PA.

Fix, David and Andy Bezener. 2000. *Birds of Northern California.* Lone Pine Publishing, Edmonton, AB.

Heintzelman, Donald S. 2001. *The Complete Backyard Birdwatcher's Home Companion.* Ragged Mountain Press, Camden, ME.

Hill, Lewis. 1991. *Secrets of Plant Propagation.* Storey Communications Inc., Pownal, VT.

Jeavons, John. 2001. *How to Grow More Vegetables.* 10 Speed Press, Berkeley, CA.

Kourik, Robert. 1997. *Pruning.* Workman Publishing Company, New York, NY.

Merilees, Bill. 1989. *Attracting Backyard Wildlife: A Guide for Nature Lovers.* Voyageur Press, Stillwater, MN.

Peirce, Pam. 2003. *Golden Gate Gardening.* Sasquatch Books, Seattle, WA.

Robinson, Peter. 1997. *Complete Guide to Water Gardening.* Reader's Digest, Westmount, PQ.

Schmidt, Marjorie G. 1980. *Growing California Native Plants.* The University of California Press, Berkeley, CA.

Tanem, Bob. 1993. *Deer Resistant Planting.* Marin County, CA. Self-published.

Tanem, Bob and Don Williamson. 2002. *Annuals for Northern California.* Lone Pine Publishing, Edmonton, AB.

Tanem, Bob and Don Williamson. 2002. *Perennials for Northern California.* Lone Pine Publishing, Edmonton, AB.

Tanem, Bob and Don Williamson. 2003. *Trees & Shrub Gardening for Northern California.* Lone Pine Publishing, Edmonton, AB.

Thompson, P. 1992. *Creative Propagation: A Grower's Guide.* Timber Press, Portland, OR.

Troetschler, Ruth, et al. 1996. *Rebugging Your Home and Garden.* PTF Press, Los Altos, CA.

ONLINE RESOURCES

Attracting Wildlife.com. How to make your backyard inviting to compatible and beneficial creatures. www.attracting-wildlife-to-your-garden.com

Berkeley Community Gardening Collaborative. Information pertaining to community gardens, school gardening programs, youth training and other gardening programs throughout California. www.ecologycenter.org/gardening/gardening.html

Beneficial Insectary. One of the largest producers and suppliers of beneficial insects used for better pest management. http://www.agrobiologicals.com/company/C258.htm

Botanique. Lists the botanical gardens in Northern California.
www.botanique.com

Bountiful Gardens. Sells untreated, open-pollinated seed of heirloom quality for vegetables, herbs, flowers, grains, green manures, compost and carbon crops.
http://www.bountifulgardens.org

California Master Gardeners Online. Advice, tips, courses and publications offered by the University of California Cooperative Extension Master Gardeners.
www.mastergardeners.org

Harmony Farm Supply and Nursery. Supplier of organic fertilizers, ecological pest controls, intergrated pest management monitoring tools and irrigation system components.
http://www.harmonyfarm.com

Horticultural, Garden Societies and Organizations. Links to most garden societies throughout the US.
http://mel.lib.mi.us/science/gardsoc.html

I love gardens. Comprehensive list of gardens to visit throughout California.
www.ilovegardens.com

Northern California, Nevada and Hawaii District of the American Rose Society. List of rose, botanical and display gardens.
www.ncnhdistrict.org/

Peaceful Valley Farm Supply. Everything you need for organic gardening.
http://www.groworganic.com

Seeds of Change. How to garden organically.
www.seedsofchange.com

SOIL TESTING FACILITIES

A&L Western Laboratories Inc.
1311 Woodland Avenue, # 1
Modesto, CA 95351
209-529-4080
http://www.al-labs-west.com/

Bolsa Analytical Laboratories
2337 Technology Parkway, Suite K
Hollister, CA 95023
831-637-4590

Caltest Analytical Laboratory
1885 North Kelly Road
Napa, CA 94558
707-258-4000
www.caltestlab.com
email: caltest@caltestlab.com

Cerco Analytical, Inc.
3942-A Valley Avenue, Suite A
Pleasanton, CA 94566-4715
925-462-2771

Environmental Technical Services
1343 Redwood Way
Petaluma, CA 94954
707-795-9605

Scientific Environmental Laboratories, Inc.
924 Industrial Avenue
Palo Alto, CA 94303
650-856-6011

Signet Testing Laboratories, Inc.
3121 Diablo Avenue
Hayward, CA 94545-2771
510-887-8484
http://www.urscorp.com

Soil and Plant Laboratory
352 Mathew Street
Santa Clara, CA 95050
408-727-0330
http://www.soilandplantlaboratory.com
email: splab7@earthlink.net

Control Laboratories
42 Hangar Way
Watsonville, CA 95076
831-724-5422
http://www.controllabs.com

HORTICULTURAL SOCIETIES

American Horticultural Society
7931 East Boulevard Drive
Alexandria, VA 22308
1-800-777-7931
http://www.ahs.org/
email: sdick@ahs.org

California Garden Clubs Incorporated
A state-wide federation of garden clubs and plant societies with over 20,000 members in over 250 garden clubs in 28 districts.
www.californiagardenclubs.org/

California Native Plant Society
2707 K Street, Suite 1
Sacramento, CA 95816-5113
916-447-2677
http://www.cnps.org
e-mail: cnps@cnps.org

GARDENS TO VISIT

Amador Flower Farm
22001 Shenandoah School Road
Plymouth, CA 95669
209-245-6660
www.amadorflowerfarm.com

Auburn Area Chamber of Commerce
Rose Gardens
601 Lincoln Way
Auburn, CA 95603
www.geocities.com/RainForest/Wetlands/
1395/publicgardens.html

Benicia Garden and Nursery
126 East E. Street
Benicia, CA 94510
707-747-9094
www.beniciagarden.com
email: Benicia@BeniciaGarden.com

Berkeley Rose Garden
Euclid Avenue between Bay View Place
and Eunice Street
Berkeley, CA 94704
510-644-6530
www.ci.berkeley.ca.us/manager/news/roses.
htm

Daffodil Hill
PO Box 756
Jackson, CA 95642
209-296-7048
www.comspark.com/daffodilhill/index.html
email: info@historicdaffodilhill.com

Filoli Gardens
86 Cañada Road
Woodside, CA 94062
650-364-8300
www.filoli.org

Fountain Square Rose Garden
7115 Greenback Lane
Citrus Heights, CA 95621
916-969-6666
http://www.sactorose.org/

Elizabeth Gamble Gardens
1431 Waverly Street
Palo Alto, CA 94301
650-329-1356
http://www.gamblegarden.org

Gardens at Heather Farm
1540 Marchbanks Drive
Walnut Creek, CA 94598
925-947-1678
http://www.gardenshf.org/

Garden Valley Ranch Nursery
498 Pepper Road
Petaluma, CA 94952
707-795-0919
www.gardenvalley.com
email: info@gardenvalley.com

Gekkeikan Japanese Gardens
1136 Sibley Street
Folsom, CA 95630
916-985-3111
www.gekkeikan-sake.com

Golden Gate Bridge South Tower
Garden and National Recreation Area
Hwys 1, 101, 880 and 280 north, south
or east of the San Francisco Bay Area.
415-921-5858 or 415-561-4700
http://www.nps.gov/goga/index.htm

Japanese Gardens
City Center Drive
North 3rd Street off Crescent Avenue
Hayward, CA 94546
http://www.ci.hayward.ca.us/communi-
ty/recreation.html
510-881-6715

Japanese Tea Garden in Golden Gate
Park
8th Avenue and Kennedy Drive
San Francisco, CA
415-752-1171
http://www.inetours.com/Pages/
SFNbrhds/Japanese_Tea_Garden.html

Luther Burbank Home and Gardens
Santa Rosa Avenue at Sonoma Avenue
Santa Rosa, CA
707-524-5445
www.parks.sonoma.net/burbank.html

Mendocino Coast Botanical Gardens
18220 North Highway One
Fort Bragg, CA 95437
707-964-4352
www.gardenbythesea.org
email: mcbg@gardenbythesea.org

McInnes Botanic Garden
Campus Arboretum of Mills College
Seminary Avenue and McArthur
Boulevard
Oakland, CA 94613
415-430-2158

Morcom Rose Gardens
(formerly Morcom Amphitheater of Rose
Gardens)
700 Jean Street
Oakland, CA 94610
510-238-3187

Quarryhill Botanical Garden
Located in the Sonoma Valley, about one-
hour north of San Francisco
Glen Ellen, CA
707-996-3802
http://www.quarryhillbg.org
e-mail: info@quarryhillbg.org

Rusch Botanical Gardens
7801 Auburn Boulevard
Citrus Heights, CA 95610
916-725-1585

Regional Parks Botanic Garden
Wildcat Canyon Road
Berkeley, CA 94708
510-841-8732
www.nativeplants.org

Ruth Bancroft Garden
1500 Bancroft Road
Walnut Creek, CA 94598-2361
925-210-9663
www.ruthbancroftgarden.org
email: info@ruthbancroftgarden.org

San Mateo Arboretum
58 Chester Way
San Mateo, CA 94402
650-579-0536

Shepard Garden and Arts Center
3330 McKinley Boulevard
Sacramento, CA 95816
916-443-9413

Stone's Iris Garden
Shake Ridge Road
Volcano, CA 95689
SE of Sacramento on Highway 88, 3
miles NE of Daffodil Hill

**Strybing Arboretum and Botanical
Gardens in Golden Gate Park**
9th Avenue at Lincoln Way
San Francisco, CA 94122
415-661-1316
www.strybing.org

Sunset Gardens and Publishing House
80 Willow Road
Menlo Park, CA 94025
415-321-3600
http://www.gardenvisit.com/ge/sunset.htm

The Blake Garden
University of California
70 Rincon Road
Berkeley, CA 94707
510-524-2449
http://www-laep.ced.berkeley.edu/laep/
blakegarden/

**The University of California Botanical
Garden**
200 Centennial Drive
Berkeley, CA 94720-5045
510-643-2755
www.botanicalgarden.berkeley.edu/

UC Davis Arboretum
University of California
One Shields Avenue
Davis, CA 95616-8526
530-752-4880
http://arboretum.ucdavis.edu/
email: arboretum@ucdavis.edu/

UC Santa Cruz Arboretum
1156 High Street
Santa Cruz 95064
831-427-2998
http://www2.ucsc.edu/arboretum

ACKNOWLEDGMENTS

We would especially like to thank our fellow garden writers Laura Peters and Alison Beck for their many contributions.

We are grateful to our principal photographers Tamara Eder and Tim Matheson and to the many people who opened their gardens for us to photograph. Many thanks to photographers Kim O'Leary and Saxon Holt and the crew of horticultural stock photographers who provided us with great pictures when we really needed them. Special thanks go to many Northern California gardens, most notably Strybing Arboretum and Botanical Gardens, Filoli Estate, Elizabeth F. Gamble Gardens, Golden Gate Park, Bonfante Gardens, Stanford University and the Japanese Friendship Gardens. We also thank VanDusen Botanical Gardens in Vancouver, B.C., the International Rose Test Garden in Portland, Oregon and Lee and Mary Grace Bertsch for allowing us to photograph their plants and gardens.

We would also like to thank Shane Kennedy, Nancy Foulds, editor Sandra Bit and designer and Master Gardener Heather Markham. Thanks also to Gerry Dotto for the cover design and to Ian Sheldon for the lovely corner flourishes that grace the pages. Others helped in various ways, close-cropping photos and providing stylistic solutions, and we thank them all.

Cover page photos:
January—hoarfrost on Dusty Miller
February—swirling *Aloe polyphylla*
March—'Addis' tulips
April— 'Monjisu Red' camellia
May—rhododendron
June—Swiss chard
July— shrub rose 'The Fairy'
August—dahlias
September—*Phormium*
October—'Orange Smoothie' pumpkins
November—'Fuyu' persimmon
December—firethorn